DANUBIAN DESTINY

Danubian Destiny

a survey Munich

Graham Hutton

Simon Publications
2003

American edition published by Little, Brown & Co. Boston
under the title: *Survey after Munich*

Library of Congress Card Number: 39007762

ISBN: 1-932512-04-7

Published by Simon Publications, Inc. P. O. Box 910455, San
Diego, CA 92191-0455

PREFACE

In 1886 a young Englishman, son of Joseph Chamberlain, was sent to Paris by his family to prepare for a career in public affairs. One day, at the École des Sciences Politiques, he heard the lecturer on diplomatic history, Albert Sorel, make this pronouncement: " On the day when the Turkish question is settled Europe will be confronted with a new problem—that of the future of the Austro-Hungarian Empire." But what perturbed young Austen Chamberlain was not the possibility that the Austro-Hungarian Monarchy might collapse and its dominions disintegrate. It was that Sorel went on to draw a conclusion most discomfiting to any thinking Englishman. The young man, destined to be Foreign Secretary of his country, heard the French professor describe the disintegration of Austria-Hungary as a possible preliminary to the break-up of the British Empire.

Sir Austen Chamberlain said that he never forgot Sorel's warning. The former Foreign Secretary of the United Kingdom was not happy about the disruption of the Austro-Hungarian political and economic unity, sanctioned by the victorious Allies in the Peace Treaties. He became towards the close of his life increasingly unhappy about the future of maimed and lamed Austria, threatened by Germany's Third Reich. But, perhaps fortunately, he did not live to see what happened to

Europe in 1938. For then what his French professor had feared half a century earlier came to pass. The last vestiges of the Austro-Hungarian Empire, the small independent states reared on its ruins and in its place, collapsed before two short and sharp German diplomatic assaults.

On the face of it, Englishmen may possibly still wonder—as no doubt young Austen Chamberlain wondered in 1886—what influence a break-up on the Danube can exert on British, or even European, destinies. But Austen Chamberlain, the student of international affairs, saw the importance of Danubia to England fifty years ago; and his last speeches to the Commons in 1937 were warnings of what might befall Britain if Germany became heir to all the Habsburgs' empire, and more besides.

This book is an endeavour to discover to what extent the Third Reich, after peaceful and spectacular victories in 1938, can mould Europe's destinies. Those victories were gained in Central Europe, the gateway to the Balkans, Russia, and the Near East. Henceforth Germany has little to fear militarily from her disrupted and disarrayed small neighbours on the farther side of the Rome-Berlin Axis. What profit the governors of the enlarged Reich can draw from that tract of country which we call 'Europe beyond Germany' must be estimated. What they can do with it and what they will do may be two very different things. But we cannot even begin to guess what they will do before we know how the entire European setting has been altered, how the disposition of European forces and resources has been changed, by German achievements in the Danubian Basin during 1938.

Accordingly this book must begin by setting out the accomplished facts. Their significance—for good or ill—must then be estimated. Such an inquiry must be undertaken dispassionately, even if we have to reckon with terrible and moving contingencies. If what Nazi Germany *will* do lies beyond the bounds of reasonable reckoning, what her rulers *can* do lies well within the bounds of calm conjecture. It is our business first to determine what they can do. After that the conclusions of author and reader may differ; and they may alike be falsified by the greatest of all imponderables in history—the hand of destiny.

The leading *motif* of this book is that a new Europe is being moulded on the farther side of the Rome-Berlin front: that from Danubian destiny will come European destiny. It may be peace or war, welfare or ill-fare. The best-laid schemes of dictators and democrats may alike go agley. But what transpires beyond the Rhine and the Alps is now bound to decide what happens to all Europeans. Nations can, of course, contract out of war; but they cannot contract out of a common destiny. And it is a common destiny which now confronts all nations in Europe.

GRAHAM HUTTON

January 1939

CONTENTS

PART I

PART II

PART III

MAPS

PART I

THE NEW DANUBIA

(i) *Introductory*

In the year 1938 two Central European dykes were burst asunder.

Austria was originally raised by Otto I a thousand years ago to protect western Christian civilization from the incursions of Tartar tribes in the south-east. It was for seven centuries the core of the Holy Roman Empire, until Napoleon ended that Empire from the west; and until 1918 Austria was the heart of a multi-racial Habsburg empire threatened by the Slavs under Russian influence and by the newly united Prussianized Germans. But Austria collapsed finally and for good in 1938. After the ancient dyke had been breached by the Nazi flood on March 12, 1938, the Danube flowed brown.

The Nazi waters gradually rose round the straggling natural barrier of another dyke, that of equally ancient Bohemia, part of Austria from 1526 to 1918. A Germany which had only been first united as a nation in 1870, which had, like an ambitious parvenu, tried before the Great War to master Austria-Hungary, and which had been defeated by a world it had challenged, had by 1938 and in five years recruited such an array of force as to burst both the dykes which preserved the Danubian Basin from a German flood.

Bismarck, uniter of the German nation by " blood and

iron," the man who did not want Austria-Hungary, with its Bohemian provinces, in his Prussianized Reich, said, " Whoever is master of Bohemia is master of Europe." After September 1938 the brown flood of Nazi-ism beat into the valleys and plains of Old Danubia—into Bohemia, Moravia, Slovakia, Ruthenia, Hungary, and Jugoslavia. A New Danubia was bound to take shape when the waters had done their work. But for the moment the landscape was unfamiliar, submerged, all ancient landmarks lost. Men lived during those tense weeks and months after Munich in taut anxiety, waiting to catch the first glimpse of other landmarks, to divine what might yet be.

The diplomatic power of the Third Reich, and the offensive might which lent German diplomacy its cogency at Munich, is based upon the necessity for the Third Reich to dominate what we call the Danubian Basin—Austria, Czecho-Slovakia, Hungary, Jugoslavia, and beyond.

There were two prior conditions which Germany had to secure before her diplomacy and her military strength could be put to the test against Britain and France at Munich. One was the military closure of her Rhine-land portals in the face of France. That was done on March 7, 1936, when the Rhineland was reoccupied and the western Locarno system unilaterally destroyed. The other was the more delicate operation—the forcible annexation of Austria without provoking Britain and France to war, or Signor Mussolini, Herr Hitler's other partner on the Rome-Berlin Axis, to quit the Axis and throw in his lot with Britain and France. This second prerequisite for the Munich Settlement was secured on March 12, 1938, when Italy was deeply involved in military commitments as far away as Spain and Ethiopia. These commitments had embroiled Italy with Britain and France; and Italy had received astute German support. Both conditions having been secured so successfully by the summer of 1938, and Italian dependence on the Rome-Berlin Axis having been ensured, the way was opened for a trial of strength, a tournament for the mastery of the Bohemian gateway to all Danubia. After an abortive trial of military strength against Czecho-Slovakia alone in the week-end of May 20, 1938—an attempt as sudden and secretive as that so successful against Austria two months earlier—the lists were prepared, accompanied by a full-dress mobilization during weeks of forearming, in the eyes of the whole world. The Czecho-Slovak fortress was delivered to Germany at Munich. European peace was saved.

For how long has that peace been saved? For what kind of Europe? At what cost—not only that cost already paid, but still to pay? On whose shoulders really rests the responsibility for keeping that peace? Answers to these anxious questions do not lie beyond the bounds of reasonable conjecture. But to hazard answers requires understanding not only of the issues at stake, but also of the national aims and interests involved, the means and methods available to realize them, the forces which must be assessed before a tentative balance of probabilities can be struck. Even when we try to compass all this the gravest question of all cannot be answered: Will the peace be kept? For as with a contract or a marriage so with peace—it takes two parties to keep it. You may be sure of yourself. But no man can be sure of another's actions.

We must therefore begin by trying to bring far-away countries a little nearer in essentials, as in the case of war they would be uncomfortably nearer than ever before in history; to discover a little more about the factors and forces which are, and have long been, influencing peoples of whom we know nothing. A new European destiny was unfolded at Munich. That is why we shall not be concerned in this book with the antecedents of that Settlement, or with arid disputation about apportionment of praise and blame. Now that we can dimly discern a few landmarks after the deluge of 1938, the job of discovering the frame to Europe's new destiny is paramount. After the deluge of 1914–18 that job lay in the hands of Britain and France alone. Now Britain and France must look far beyond the Rhine frontiers, beyond the spot where in 1934 Lord Baldwin placed England's frontiers, to the yet undefined and perhaps indefinite frontiers of the Third Reich and its confederates somewhere along the Danube. To what end, in what direction, will Germany turn the resources of those far-away countries, and the peoples of whom we know nothing, which were pawned to provide another instalment for peace? What are the bounds of her legitimate interests there? Can she erect and buttress a Third Reich stretching from the mouth of the Rhine to the mouth of the Danube? Will all her resources enable her to do it? If so, will it be mightier for war, or will her war-potency be weakened in striving to accomplish the task? How fast and with what degree of self-sufficiency can she achieve it? What *rôles* in the drama will be played by the countries in her way, as well as those still out of it?

Events in Central Europe during 1938 have raised these questions. The answers must henceforth be sought where the queries arose: in the Danubian Basin.

(ii) *Backcloth to Munich*

Europe is divided by two great rivers whose waters almost mingle at the source—the Rhine and the Danube. Across these two great rivers the Roman civilization of the west had to face barbarian tribes whose descendants eventually broke up the Empire into new tribal nations. For many centuries so much inter-tribal fighting went on that men might well have concluded that, after the irruptions of Goths and Franks and Lombards and Slavs and Magyars from the farther side of Rhine and Danube, neither those rivers nor the great Alpine, Dalmatian, Pyrenean, or Carpathian mountain-ranges would thenceforth play any important *rôle* in fashioning the destinies of Europe's future nations.

The Rhine and the Alps gradually came to demarcate fairly clearly the Germans from the French and the Italians; but the Danube, flowing through gorges and great plains, through gaps between Alps and Bohemian Forest heights, between Carpathians and Balkans, across the vast Hungarian and Rumanian plains, ran through countries in which lived a congeries of peoples. Scarcely a single clear line could be discovered between Germans,

Czechs, Slovaks, Hungarians (Magyars), Croats, Serbs, Rumans, Ruthenes, Bulgars, and even Russians and Greeks. Moreover, for five centuries the Turks ruled the Balkan Peninsula and the Lower Danube; and, while the nascent nations of the west were able to develop at home and overseas, the peoples east and south-east of Vienna were held down, held back. The Holy Roman Empire had begun by trying to weld Franks and Lombards and Latins and Germans into some semblance of unity, had continually built up vast ramshackle realms, only to see them distintegrate because of wide disparities and distances and the impossibility of clamping centralized administration on the local feudal nobles, and had finally been forced to abandon the attempt to unify Germany. The Empire thus came to be an elective association of mainly German-speaking nobles and kings, bound only by the weakest of all feudal ties—that between many powerful rulers on one side and one of their elected number, the Emperor alone, on the other.

Intrigues and diplomatic marriages destroyed the electoral basis of the Empire. Eventually it came into the hereditary hands of one of the noble families, the Habsburgs. While Germany's states and small principalities were torn by the Reformation, and retarded by the Thirty Years War to which it led, the Holy Roman Empire possessed a solid territorial core in Austria. It was also solidly Catholic. In the eighteenth century, when France and Britain were consolidating overseas possessions into great empires, the Habsburgs, already ruling over Czechs and Slovaks and Hungarians, began that reversal of former movements in South-eastern

Europe which in the next century became known as
" turning the Turks out of Europe, bag and baggage."
The Turkish tide was turned; and from beneath it
appeared, like sand covered with storm-wrack, one small
people after another—tribe by tribe, folk by folk, here
preserved with language and dress and customs in mountain valleys, there protected from the Turkish flood by
having taken to the high mountains.

The Turks, cruel though they often were for a few
months, were not on the whole bad masters; they were
good administrators; they allowed, again on the whole,
freedom of religious cult, dress, language, customs, to
their Christian subjects. Thus the nineteenth century,
beginning with Napoleon's forcible termination of the
Holy Roman Empire in 1806 and the voluntary prefer-
ence of the last Emperor (Francis II) for the title
" Hereditary Emperor of Austria," brought an ebbing of
the tide of conquest from Central and South-eastern
Europe. Beginning in Greece, the movement for libera-
tion, itself liberated by the French Revolution, took root
in Serbia, Rumania (Wallachia-Moldavia), Montenegro,
Albania, Bulgaria. Austrians and Hungarians, the two
uneasy partners in the Austrian Empire, first settled their
own differences in the Compromise of 1867 after
Austria's defeat by Bismarck in 1866. Thereafter the
German Reich of Bismarck forced the Austro-Hungarian
monarchy to look on all Europe to the east and south
of it as its private preserve. Just as Bismarck pushed
Austria-Hungary south-eastward out of the new Reich's
path, so he pushed defeated France, after 1870, into
North Africa (especially Tunisia).

But as the Turkish tide receded more than the small submerged peoples of the peninsula began to appear. Great Powers began to show that they too had conflicting interests in the Danubian Basin. Austria-Hungary was not left alone to obtain the Turks' reversion. Prussia, having defeated Austria in 1866 and France in 1870, began to emphasize the need of all Germans for unity of policy. Though Bismarck did not want to embrace what he called "degenerate Austrians" in the new-united Germany, other Germans—at the outset especially a movement in the German districts of Bohemia (Austrian Sudetenland) and round Vienna which was known as Pan-German—badly wanted to abolish the separate Austria and build up one vast German Reich, like the old Holy Roman Empire of the first German Emperors. This Pan-German, anti-Semitic, anti-Habsburg movement became stronger in Austria (not Hungary, which was a separate Magyar kingdom under the 1867 Compromise) after the new, young German Emperor, William II, " dropped the pilot," Bismarck, at the close of the eighties of last century. But it met another ' pan ' movement—and met it head on, inside Austrian dominions. This was the Pan-Slav movement, sponsored by Russia.

As the Turks retreated towards Constantinople, and as the power of Vienna followed them into the Balkan Peninsula, the ambitions of the Czars also were directed towards the Near East, towards the Straits and the warm-water harbours which could defy that greatest ally of Russia's foes, General Winter. Thus the new small nations which were being born from what had so long been a Turkish matrix—Greece, Serbia, Rumania, Bulgaria, Montenegro, and Albania—took up positions on the mountainous rim around the Danubian Basin. That basin and its contents became the goal of a struggle between, primarily, Austrians and Hungarians on the one side and all the Slavs, backed by Russia, on the other—that is, Teuton *versus* Slav in the Danubian arena. As the united power of Vienna and Budapest encroached on the Southern Slavs' territories—beginning from the Slav lands of Croats and Slovenes in the north and working down through Bosnia and Herzegovina towards the domination of the Dalmatian coast—so the new independent Slav and Ruman nations—Serbia, Montenegro, Albania, Bulgaria, and Rumania—tended to look towards Russia for aid. In 1903 an attempt was made to regulate Austrian and Russian interests in the Danubian arena. But it failed. When, finally, Austria-Hungary decided openly to annex Bosnia-Herzegovina in 1908, the Serbs, the brothers of the Croats and Slovenes, found themselves facing Hungary on almost all sides. In the meantime, as we now have fatal cause to know, a mighty united Germany, reversing Bismarck's policy of " hands off Austria " and " friendship with England," was challenging England for sea-power at the same time as it was seeking to dominate Vienna. The pre-War policy of William II and his nearest advisers was to keep Austria-Hungary as a German sphere of influence, to strengthen it and expand its influence into the Balkans on behalf of a German drive to the south-east, whose ultimate goal was to be the Middle East and Bagdad. In doing this Germany necessarily had to try to prevent two important and hostile junctions of Great Powers. One had already taken place since the turn of the century—the junction of France in the west with Czarist Russia in the east. That was always the nightmare of the famous Prussian General Staff—the fear lest Germany be beset on both flanks. The other junction—less obvious, not yet achieved, but more dangerous in the long run to all Germany's and Austria-Hungary's ambitions—was the junction of Russia with the southern and south-eastern Slav nations round the rim of the Danubian Basin. Thus, willy-nilly, the German Reich was forced to buttress Austria-Hungary. It was buttressing the ramshackle but astonishingly successful Habsburg dominions, with their minority of Austrian Germans and their overwhelming majority of non-Germans— Magyars (partners in ruling the state), and then Czechs, Slovaks, Ruthenes or Ukrainian Russians, Rumans, Croats, Slovenes, Bosniak Serbs—and everywhere the Jews. In lending aid and support to Vienna and Budapest, aid that was always received (even in critical moments, as in 1908, when Austria-Hungary pocketed Bosnia and Herzegovina) with misgivings, Berlin was gradually making enemies of Russia, France, and England.

It was, of course, the so-called Eastern Question—the problem of what to do with the territories vacated by the Turk, Europe's " sick man "—that led to the Balkan Wars and their immediate aftermath, the Great War. Austria-Hungary and Russia claimed the sick man's estate. The small tenants were bartered about like pawns, despite their new nationhood. England and

France feared either solution—Russian power at Constantinople and in the Balkans, or Austro-Hungarian, if Austro-Hungarian really meant German—and so did nothing but try to stabilize an inherently unstable situation. Finally, Germany was egging Austria-Hungary on in a direction which an ill-advised group in Vienna wanted only too well to take: the destruction of Serbia before Russia, Rumania, and Bulgaria could make a united *bloc* with her to stem the Teutonic advance into the peninsula. Thus, viewed from the historical angle, the Great War was unleashed mainly because of a rivalry between three Great Powers to dominate the entire Danubian Basin. The Austro-Hungarian monarchy thought itself divinely appointed for that task. Behind it stood the Reich reared by Bismarck, now led by William II and his unskilful lieutenants. Their ultimate aim was to give Austria-Hungary an apparent victory over Serbia, only the better to control Austria-Hungary herself with all her dominions. In this way, then, even pre-War Germany was intent upon achieving a unity between all German-speaking peoples. It was not, however, conceived as a vast empire, though many German dreamers wrote of it as such. It was (perhaps wisely) planned as a German-Austrian-Hungarian condominium over the Danube—but not that Danube known to Austrians and Hungarians, flowing into the lesser-known lands of the Balkans. Rather was the new German confederation to dominate all the Danubian Basin—from the source of the Danube near the Rhine, through Germany proper, through Austria and Hungary, with their tributaries running up into Bohemia and Slovakia and down into the Dalmatian mountains, and so into Bulgaria and Rumania, to the Black Sea, Constantinople, the Straits, and the Middle East.

It is important that we should not, in the storm and stress of current or recent events, forget the lessons of that critical decade which preceded 1914. For the crises which broke out over races in naval armament, over North African colonies and Spain, over Austria and the drive to the south-east, over Franco-Russian alliances and the growing pressure of Germans upon Slavs, have been repeated in our own days with discomfiting precision and more violent methods. Then, as now, the fear about peace, rather than war, was lest confederate Germany, Austria, and Hungary, containing Czecho-Slovakia (as it came to be called), would utilize peaceful territorial gains in order to organize a vast Reich for war purposes. Indeed, this was the underlying motive of the warning memorandum to the British authorities by Sir Eyre Crowe in 1907. Even before 1914 it was freely remarked that, though Germany and Austria-Hungary might not want war, once they had together gained dominion over the entire Danubian Basin their diplomacy would be backed by such military might and economic resources that the two Western Powers alone could not combat that combination.

The Triple Entente—England, France, Russia—was the practical expression of this fear. Its consolidation during the Balkan Wars, and its immediate entry into effect in 1914 when Germany and Austria-Hungary had stood adamant over the Austro-Hungarian ultimatum to Serbia, was evidence that in reality the non-German

Great Powers had decided that the risk of so large a German Empire athwart all Europe was too considerable to be borne in peace.

But the post-War settlement of Europe, despite the much-maligned Treaty of Versailles, actually turned out more favourable to the German peoples of Europe than seemed possible at the outset. First, Russia had gone Bolshevik, and was therefore anathema to the Governments of Germany's western neighbours. Germany, the German Republic of Weimar based on Social Democracy, was quick to conclude the Treaty of Rapallo with Soviet Russia. Secondly, no other small Slav nation was even governed by Socialists, while those parts of pre-War Russia which had now become independent nations—Poland, Finland, Estonia, Latvia, Lithuania—eyed their late masters, now Communists, with the deepest mistrust across new common frontiers. Thirdly, the Allies had decimated the Austro-Hungarian Empire, and in so doing had taken away from Austria the ability and even the will to maintain a separate existence. Austria herself wanted to join with Germany as a federated state after the terms of the Peace Treaties became known, for both that Germany and that small Austria were governed by Social Democrats, and both were republics. The Allies stopped it by lending Austria money on condition she did not join Germany; but they could not lend her the necessary strength to rally to herself all the peoples and resources of the new and independent states, or the old but now enlarged states, which the Allies had scooped out of the Danubian Basin. Austria's rulers, her bankers, her industrialists, her armies, had once dominated that basin. Czecho-Slovakia, Hungary, Rumania, Poland, Jugoslavia, Italy—all these were either created or enlarged by dissection of the Habsburg empire. Their heady nationalism found political expression in passionate hatreds destined to last a score of years, found economic expression in such trade barriers as reduced their mutual dependence to a minimum, stimulated unnecessary and uneconomic production inside each state, and so robbed Vienna of its hope to lead a peacefully and voluntarily recreated Danubian Federation.

Thus, once the Republic of Weimar had given place to the Third Reich of Brownshirts and Blackshirts, Germany's opportunity arose.

In as short a five years as history can ever have witnessed Nazi Germany not only rearmed to such a degree as to enable her diplomacy by fearful threats to be victorious over all others, but she was also able to exploit to the full the divisions among her potential adversaries. Bismarck's successors in the Second Reich had thrown away all their chances by ignoring his cardinal policy of affording himself only one adversary at a time. Herr Hitler and his advisers built up the Third Reich by reverting to Bismarck's policy Yet they did so to achieve aims other than Bismarck's. Methodically, and in stages corresponding to the strength of their threatening armaments at the moment, they set about the closing of the Rhine frontier in the face of France (March 7, 1936); they played off Italy against France, and France against Britain, over the Spanish question; and when in Spain and Ethiopia Signor Mussolini was tied up and dependent on Germany they forcibly incorporated Austria in the Reich (March 12, 1938). From that to the equally forcible incorporation of Czecho-Slovak territories, the dismemberment of Czecho-Slovakia's territory, and the reduction of the remainder to utter dependence on the Third Reich, was only a short if risky step. If Austria after centuries of historic distinction from Prussia and Germany could justifiably be made part of the new Pan-German Reich, why not Czecho-Slovakia? Czecho-Slovakia was wholly created out of Austria-Hungary; and once the Empire which in pre-War days had dominated the Danubian Basin had been dissected by the Allies, why should not Germany incorporate, either utterly or by forcible federation (as in the case of the new Czecho-Slovakia), Hungary and Jugoslavia and Rumania in her new Danubian confederacy?

Naturally this process, undertaken by a Third Reich infinitely more potent for war and infinitely less trammelled by principles than the Kaiser's Second Reich, would make utter and futile nonsense of the war to end wars, the Great War of 1914–18 to make the world safe for democracy, the war for the self-determination of small nations. But war is, perhaps, always nonsense, though not always futile. And perhaps the Third Reich, embracing all Europe's Germans, washed by Rhine and Danube from North Sea to Black Sea, dominating in vanished Austria's place the Danubian Basin and all its materials and men, may, in gaining by mere threat of war what the Great War was fought to prevent, give Europe peace in our time.

Is it peace in our time? And if not, how is the beam of the European balance likely to tilt?

It is to answer in part—which is all that is possible—these, the most vexed queries of our time, that we must look at the new Danubian Empire which the Third Reich has already half erected. Throughout the centuries, as barely a generation ago, the great convulsions of European history have swayed back and forth along the Rhine-Danube axis of our continent. Once more we are faced with a struggle, a struggle which has hitherto gone on in a time of so-called peace, but a struggle of which the outcome will decide the fate of Europe—indeed, perhaps of the world—in what remains of the twentieth century.

Like Marlborough at the beginning of the eighteenth century, we turn our eyes to the Rhine and the Danube. Like Englishmen at the beginning of the nineteenth century, hearing the news of the end of the Holy Roman Empire, we look again towards Danube and Rhine. In the twentieth century we try to pierce a mist of terrible uncertainties. The war of 1914–18 looks futile. The peace which ended it is almost itself ended. We have been worsted in diplomacy because we are once more bound to the Continent by invisible, but terribly potent, aerial bonds; and again our regard travels beyond the Rhine-Danube axis—not, indeed, to any other axis, however vaunted. What has happened, and what is being brewed, in the Danubian Basin?

(iii) *The New Central Europe*

Within six months of 1938 Austria had disappeared from the map, and a rump Czecho-Slovakia, monstrously misshapen, sprawled between a greatly enlarged Germany, Poland, and Hungary. It is useful to assess the effects of the two German alterations in the map of Central Europe in March and September of 1938 as if they had been one. In fact, of course, they were but two stages in one process. We can begin by describing the geographical changes and their importance before passing to consider changes in distribution of population, military strength, and economic power.

The incorporation of Austria in Germany gave the Third Reich a common frontier with its partner on the Rome-Berlin Axis. Within twelve hours of the overthrow of Dr Schuschnigg's Government in Vienna German motorized troops appeared at the Italian frontier-post at the summit of the Brenner Pass. The frontier of the Reich with Switzerland was almost doubled; and at such a point that a future German thrust up the Rhine towards its source would obtain control not only of the former Austrian South Tirol (now the Italian Alto Adige), but also of the Italian-speaking Swiss Ticino, so long coveted by Italy herself. Germany obtained control of the centuries-old trade route from Vienna to Venice, across the Semmering Pass, through Klagenfurt, Villach, across the Carnic Alps, and down the valleys of the Tagliamento and Piave rivers. Into German hands fell two more new common frontiers, one with Jugoslavia and one with Hungary. That with Jugoslavia constituted a further threat to Italy, for across a narrow neck of Jugoslav territory lies the former Austrian port of Trieste. It is only 75 miles now from German territory to Trieste. As to Jugoslavia herself, her new common frontier with

Germany runs right across the pre-War Austrian provinces of Styria and Carniola, parts of which she obtained from Austria. South of them, in Jugoslavia, lie the lands of the Croats, formerly part of Hungary; and the Croats, strong Catholics, have long looked more favourably on Vienna than on Budapest or Belgrade. Vienna is now German, which raises problems for Belgrade. As to Germany's new common frontier with Hungary, this is of all the least militarily defensible. It runs across country as flat as a Hungarian pancake. The last foothills of the great Alpine mass turn due northward after completing the German-Jugoslav frontier; and, save for the isolated hills of the Bakony forest in the Hungarian Plain and the foothills of the Carpathians that straggle down almost to Budapest, there are now no mountains between Vienna and the Transylvanian Alps of Rumania. The Great Hungarian Plain, part of the greater plain that stretches into the heart of Europe from the Asiatic steppes, lies open before Germany, leading towards a Transylvania which before the War was part of Hungary and is now Rumanian.

The annexation of Austria in March 1938 altered one last frontier—but only for six months. This was the German frontier with Czecho-Slovakia. Of all Germany's frontiers, both before and after March of 1938, this was the most important. First, the diamond-shaped natural stronghold of Bohemia and Moravia had throughout the centuries been either the frontier outpost of Austria or else, before that, the independent kingdom of Bohemia. The German-speaking peoples established inside that stronghold were descended from the skilled

CENTRAL EUROPE, JANUARY 1938

To avoid confusion of
been given only in the f
only in

THE SAME, JANUARY 1939

physical features have
...p and names of towns
...econd.

workmen invited to settle there by the old Czech kings of Bohemia; and they settled there in an age when nations, nationality, and nationalism had little meaning, feudal rights and duties being stronger than national rights and duties. Accordingly the international body of experts advising the Allies at the Peace Conference unanimously recommended that the new Czecho-Slovakia, having gained its independence from the Habsburg Austria to which it had lost it three centuries earlier, should be given frontiers with Germany and Austria corresponding to the limits of the crownlands of ancient Bohemia. The reasons were not a pious respect for historical tradition, but economic necessity based on vital communications and military necessity based on Czecho-Slovakia's need to hold against all comers the mountain-girt limits of her ancient home. Consequently when post-War Austria was whisked from the map of Europe the German Reich's frontiers ran almost round Czecho-Slovakia, from the Silesian junction between Poland, Germany, and Czecho-Slovakia in the north, round Saxony, Bavaria, and Austria, to Bratislava (Pressburg), capital of Slovakia and junction between the new Germany, Hungary, and Slovakia.

Secondly, however, while Bohemia and Moravia within the walls of the Bohemian Forest and the Ore Mountains are flatter than any other parts of the country, Slovakia and Ruthenia, the two eastern provinces of Czecho-Slovakia, are hilly and mountainous, with little first-class agricultural land. Germany with Austria so surrounded Bohemia and Moravia that the German pincers threatened to cut Bohemia and Moravia from Slovakia and Ruthenia, along the line of the Little Carpathians between Opava (Troppau) and Bratislava.

Thirdly, the annexation of Austria was bound to give the Third Reich control of all routes, by road, river, and rail, from Czecho-Slovakia towards the west. Vienna was the centre of communications in the Habsburg Monarchy. Its control by Germany left to Prague only one reasonably direct route for supplies outside German control—the Polish railway from Silesia to Gdynia. Moreover, if the Third Reich could contrive to dismember Czecho-Slovakia peaceably, then the natural frontiers formed by the cordon of high mountains might be taken by Germany. In that case all the vital defences and economic communications of the Czecho-Slovakia created in 1919 would pass into German hands.

At this point let us examine the geographical changes brought about by the Munich Settlement and by the International Commission of Ambassadors in Berlin set up under that Settlement. The Commission, composed of an Under-Secretary in the German Foreign Office, the Italian, French, and British Ambassadors in Berlin, and a representative of Czecho-Slovakia, proceeded to dismember Czecho-Slovakia according to the German plan. The Munich meeting was held on September 29, 1938. Already, on September 21, both the Polish and the Hungarian Governments had put forward claims in London to the effect that whatever method be devised for dealing with Germany's claims on behalf of German-speaking minorities in Czecho-Slovakia should also be applied to the Polish and Hungarian minorities there. When the Czecho-Slovak representatives at Munich were handed the terms of the Settlement it was found that (a) the Polish and Hungarian claims were to be left to Czecho-Slovakia, Poland, and Hungary to settle inside three months, that (b) if they were not then settled the four Great Powers would meet again, and that (c) Germany and Italy would give no guarantee of the new Czecho-Slovak frontiers until the Polish and Hungarian claims were settled. Accordingly, the Government of the rump Czecho-Slovakia, having lost its capacity for self-defence by the German occupation of the first zones on October 1 and 2, had no choice but to conform to the desires of the Poles and the Hungarians. On September 30, the day after Munich, the Polish Government sent an ultimatum, described as a Note having "an ultimatum character," to the Czecho-Slovak Government; and on October 1 the Czecho-Slovak Cabinet agreed to the Poles' demands. On October 2 Polish troops occupied the first zone of Teschen, the town over which disputations had continued between Poland and Czecho-Slovakia ever since the War. Within a few days they also occupied Bohumin—the most important railway junction of Eastern Europe.

The Hungarians' demands on Czecho-Slovakia took longer to discuss, and a settlement was protracted beyond the time taken by Germany and Poland, owing to the lack of military strength on the part of Hungary. But by November 10 Hungarian troops had occupied many Slovak and Ruthene territories. These were awarded to Hungary under a German-Italian arbitration at Vienna in October-November.

The outcome of the Munich Settlement, as far as the

new frontiers of Germany and Czecho-Slovakia were concerned, was, therefore, far-reaching. It altered the territorial bounds of Germany, Czecho-Slovakia, Hungary, and Poland.

First, the boundaries of the new German districts transferred the Bohemian and Moravian mountain barriers into German hands. Czecho-Slovakia's natural frontiers disappeared along with her man-made defences. The waist of the country, across Moravia, was cut down from 140 to 65 miles—the pincers came closer than ever together. Germany went beyond the claims put in writing at Godesberg, and occupied, under bilateral agreement with the Government in Prague, non-German districts in Bohemia. The small town of Theblen and the village of Devin, on the Slovak side of the Danube and of its tributary, the March (the frontier between old Austria and Czecho-Slovakia), were suddenly occupied by Germany, again by bilateral agreement with Prague, at the end of November 1938. This gave Germany the bridgehead on the Slovak side of the Danube, in the rear of the strategically important Slovak capital, Bratislava. But it also gave her control of that city, which, under the Magyar name Pozsony, the Hungarians were claiming because it was the coronation city of the old Hungarian kings. Finally, in November, Germany obtained cession of a strip of territory from the Prague Government, 60 yards wide and 65 miles long, right across the waist of the remaining Czecho-Slovak territory, for construction of a motor-road from Breslau, in the north, to Vienna, in the south. This strip was to be German territory, policed and patrolled by German officers. Such a cession by one nominally sovereign state to another was virtually unprecedented.

Polish troops, when occupying the agreed zones round Teschen, pushed on to occupy territory even beyond the strategic railway junction of Bohumin, the nodal traffic point in the Silesian triangle between Poland, Germany, and Czecho-Slovakia. Elsewhere (for example, along the northern Slovak frontier) small cessions were made to Poland. Here, before the War, the Habsburg Monarchy had been in possession of the Galician foothills and Ukrainian plain on the farther side of the Carpathians. Poland's gains after Munich gave her a stronger hold on her 700-mile-long frontier with Czecho-Slovakia—and precisely at the point where she might have reason, in the event of a future Polish-German dispute, to need the railways and resources she obtained.

Hungary obtained from Slovakia and Ruthenia the most desirable portions of those territories which, before the War, had belonged to her. She did not obtain Pozsony (Bratislava or Pressburg), the capital of Slovakia, owing to opposition by Germany; the reasons for this will appear when we examine the strategic and economic effects of the Munich Settlement (see pp. 70–119). But she was able to obtain the return of the rich Csallóköz, or Grosse Schütt Island, formed by the branching Danube between Bratislava and Komárom, and a long strip of territory, mainly populated by Magyars, stretching from slightly east of Bratislava, through the towns of Losonc (Lucenec) and Kassa (Kosice) in Slovakia, and through the chief towns of Ruthenia, Ungvár (Uzhorod), Munkács (Munkacevo), and Beregszász (Berehovo).

This entire strip comprised the most fertile portions of Slovakia, since, lying along the former Hungarian frontier, it was composed mainly of the plains and valleys below the arch of the Carpathians and their southward-branching foothills. The Hungarian frontier with Rumania was lengthened by some 15 miles, as Hungary's frontier at its north-eastern tip was extended by acquisitions from Ruthenia. The only fertile portions of Ruthenia—Sub-Carpatho-Russia, as it was called when it formed part of Czecho-Slovakia, and Carpatho-Ukraine, as the Germans now call it—went to Hungary, for the former province of Czecho-Slovakia is the most mountainous and the least advanced in economic or social development. Consequently the deprivation of all its valleys and their towns—valleys which, be it said, had before the War developed their trade in the natural southward direction to Budapest—left Ruthenia with little hope of economic redressment, either by its own efforts or by those of the equally severely maimed Czecho-Slovakia, to which what was left belonged.

In redrawing the map of Central Europe Germany and her associates at Munich and thereafter did not alter the existing frontiers of Germany with Italy, Jugoslavia, or Hungary. The post-War frontiers of former Austria were left as they were settled either in the Treaty of Saint-Germain or in the results of the Burgenland plebiscite of 1921. Herr Hitler during his visit to Italy in May 1938 renounced (on veiled conditions) his claims, never yet preferred, to the South Tirol, taken by Italy after the War. The Polish Corridor remained as a gap between Germany proper and East Prussia. A rump

Czecho-Slovak state, including a scarcely durable Ruthenia or Carpatho-Ukraine, was kept in being; it was not reincorporated in the now-united German Reich, though its pre-War overlords in Austria had been absorbed into Germany. Two Adriatic harbours, seized by Italy after the War and belonging respectively to Austria and Hungary before it—Trieste and Fiume— were not claimed by Germany in her new capacity as heir to pre-War Austria-Hungary. Nor did she claim the northern Slovene and Croat territories of Jugoslavia, which had been taken from Austria and Hungary after the War. Czecho-Slovakia alone, at least for the moment, was dismembered; and this in favour of Poland and Hungary as much as in favour of the Third Reich.

That, then, is the map of the New Danubia in strictly geographical terms. Let us go on to see what these geographical changes meant in terms of population.

(iv) *The Peoples of the New Danubia*

Czecho-Slovakia, which lost 29 per cent. of her territory after Munich, lost 33 per cent. of her inhabitants. The population of Czecho-Slovakia before Munich was just under 15,000,000 souls. Of these, the Munich Settlement and its associated agreements took away more than 4,800,000. Of these, 3,700,000 were incorporated in Germany, among them being about 750,000 pure Czechs. A further 260,000 persons went to Poland; among these, apart from the 120,000 more or less demonstrable Poles, were over 100,000 Czechs and Slovaks, as well as some Germans. Finally, about

900,000 persons went to Hungary, of whom about 200,000 were Czechs, Slovaks, and Ruthenes, and almost one-half Jews and non-Aryans.

The new purely Czech territories—that is, Bohemia and Moravia-Silesia alone—were reduced from a population of about 11,000,000 souls to one of less than 7,000,000. The two remaining provinces, Slovakia and Ruthenia together, found their population cut down from its 1930 figure of just over 4,000,000 to just over 3,000,000. Thus more than 1,000,000 Czechs, Slovaks, and Ruthenes were handed over as new national minorities within the countries obtaining sections of old Czecho-Slovakia—namely, Germany, Poland, and Hungary. On the other hand, it is estimated that inside the new Czecho-Slovakia there are still about 250,000 Germans and some 50,000 Hungarians. This is because cities situated in undeniable Czech or Slovak territory— for example, Prague, Brno (Brünn), Plzen (Pilsen), Bratislava (Pressburg, Pozsony), Nitra (Nyitra)—have German or Hungarian populations beside Czech or Slovak. The upshot of the Post-Munich Settlement was that, while Germany and her associates obtained more territory than they were entitled to, either on strict ethnographical grounds or on the letter of the Godesberg and Munich plans, new minorities were created alongside the old. The new Czecho-Slovakia's population, at under 10,000,000 souls, was made more dependent on agriculture and deprived of its renowned industrial resources, at the same time as Slovakia and Ruthenia were bereft by Hungary of their only fertile regions. Accordingly pressure of the new state's population on natural resources was intensified by the Munich Settlement; and the preponderance of Czechs over Slovaks and Ruthenes has been altered in favour of the latter two groups.

A word must be said about the Jews. In all the East, Central, and South-east European countries there are many Jews. It has been calculated that, defined racially and not by religion *practised*, there are about 10,000,000 Jews or part-Jews in these countries alone. The position of these people is now pathetic. For generations before the War the great empires on the Continent—those of the Czars, Habsburg Emperors, and Prusso-German Emperors—pursued policies which aimed at assimilating the intellectual, non-practising Jews as good Germans, Austrians, Hungarians, or Russians. In census after census such Jews were inscribed as Germans, Austrians or Magyars, and Russians. Now nobody wants the Jews; every Government east of the Rhine and south of the Alps has passed or is passing anti-Semitic legislation, aimed at eradication of Jews from the national stock, cultural and commercial life, universities, etc. Sometimes, as in Hungary or Italy, a Jew is defined by reference to the date of his baptism—for example, those baptized before 1919 not being reckoned Jews. Or he can lose the stigma of Jewry because of his length of service to the State. Often, however—and Germany is the most striking example—anyone who is not a hundred per cent. 'Aryan' is defined and treated (or maltreated) as a Jew. By limitation of entry to universities (*numerus clausus* system) and professions, by exclusion from many activities, by resuscitation of the stigma of the medieval ghetto, and by brute violence, Jews in many Continental countries beyond the Rhine are being remorselessly ground out of existence, without any possibility of fleeing to another country or continent. Even if they could their property is sequestrated in the country in which they have hitherto been full citizens. Then other countries are approached for financial or commercial concessions to the Jew-baiting country, ostensibly to 'help the Jews' to unfreeze their impounded property.

The significance of Munich in this connexion is that it gave an enormous impetus to anti-Semitism throughout Europe beyond Germany in convincing all Germany's neighbours that the harbouring or good treatment of Jews would be taken by the Nazis for unrighteousness. Thus in Hungary, Poland, Italy, Jugoslavia, Rumania, and in the new Czecho-Slovakia a wave of anti-Semitism was thrown up. As on local racial definition there are over 500,000 Jews in the new Czecho-Slovakia, over 750,000 in Hungary, nearly 1,500,000 in Rumania, and 2,000,000 in Poland, the magnitude of the problem, both social and economic, can be gauged. The protection afforded to Christianized Jews by the Roman Catholic Church, the attack of the totalitarian State upon all Churches, the struggles over the State's claim to control the training of children— all these trends, as familiar to us on the Russian scene as on the German, are now being intensified throughout Danubia. A new clash between races, sects, generations, Churches, and the State has been rendered inevitable throughout Central and Balkan Europe. The struggle is being unfolded inside each country; but its development can only weaken each small country's national unity, paralyse its population as a whole, and so play into the hands of the leading exponents of totalitarian social policy—Nazi Germany.

After Munich there are still 5,500,000 Germans living in neighbouring countries, exclusive of such Teutonic peoples as the Scandinavians, Dutch, Flemings, and German-Swiss. To be fair to Germany, we will include *all* German-speaking Alsatians or Lorrainers—that is, 1,450,000, as contrasted with the German claim of 1,700,000—in this total. The 5,500,000 are distributed roughly in this fashion: 1,450,000 in France (Alsace-Lorraine); 500,000 in Hungary (Suabians, Saxons); 250,000 in Czecho-Slovakia; 800,000 in Rumania (Transylvanian Saxons); 900,000 in Poland (Prussians, Silesians, Saxons); 750,000 in Jugoslavia, Albania, Bulgaria, and Greece (Austrians, Saxons, Suabians); 250,000 in the Baltic states, Finland, and the three Scandinavian kingdoms (Balts, Prussians, Saxons); 250,000 throughout Russia (the Don Saxons, Balts, Prussians); and—few but important—about 250,000 in Italy (Austrians in the South Tirol, Venezia Giulia, Istria). The Nazi experts contrive to make even this 5,500,000 into 9,000,000. Of course, if the Danes, Swedes, Norwegians, Dutch, Flemings, German-Swiss, and other such 'Nordics' or 'Aryans' are to be placed under the protection of the Third Reich on grounds of their essential 'Germanism,' this 5,500,000 of Germans outside the Reich could be swollen by another 20,000,000, making 25,500,000 'Nordics' or Nazi-defined 'Germans' beyond the post-

Munich bounds of the Third Reich. The population of the Reich in 1938 alone jumped from just over 68,000,000 to practically 80,000,000—in virtue of the annexations of Austrian and Czecho-Slovak territory—and the Third Reich has now a practically united territory for its 80,000,000 souls, save only in the case of East Prussia and Danzig, separated from the Reich by the Polish Corridor. The number of real Germans living in states that have a common frontier with the Reich, and that therefore might in future be forced to give land and German citizens to Germany, is still over 4,000,000. In this total we should include the 800,000 Germans in Rumania, because the new Czecho-Slovakia is under German domination, and its common frontier with Rumania must be reckoned as one of Germany's own frontiers.

Beyond the present[1] bounds of the Third Reich, therefore, there are living in Europe, *excluding* Russia, about 5,250,000 Germans, 20,000,000 Teutonic peoples, 42,000,000 Italians, 31,000,000 Spanish and Portuguese, 42,000,000 French, 48,000,000 British and Irish, 85,000,000 Slav peoples, 14,000,000 Finns and Hungarians, and about 5,000,000 others—Turks, Albanians, etc. These figures give us a rough national or racial division on the following lines: 106,250,000 Germans, including what we may call para-Germans; 85,000,000 Slavs outside Russia-in-Europe, which has a common frontier with 50 out of these 85 millions; and France, Italy, and Great Britain all equal, with populations between 42 and 45 millions. On the outer rim of Europe

[1] January 1, 1939.

come the 31,000,000 Spaniards and Portuguese, Latins
for the most part; and many Rumanians, Turks, Greeks,
and Albanians. Right in the centre of Europe are now
10,000,000 Magyars in a compact state, and in the north
are their equally non-Indo-Aryan cousins, the 4,500,000
Finns and Estonians.

The Latin populations are split between the opposing
political and ideological systems of France and Italy,
with Latin Spain and Portugal a bone of contention
between them. If Latin France agrees to allow Latin
Italy to instal herself and Germany in a Fascist Spain,
then the European Latins will be divided into 70,000,000
or more Italians, Spaniards, and Portuguese on the
totalitarian Right Wing, and France's 42,000,000 on the
democratic, western front.

These population figures are important, for it is not
generally realized that politics reflect the clashes between
masses of populations. For example, the ideological
division of Europe after Munich, expressed in terms of
peoples, presents a serious aspect to Britain and France.
The two Western Powers can muster in their European
dominions a total of 90,000,000 souls. If Spain, Italy,
Germany, and Germany's Central European dominions
of Hungary and Czecho-Slovakia are ranged solidly together, they can command 170,000,000. If Poland,
Rumania, Jugoslavia, and the smaller Central and
South-east European countries be added to them they
will muster 240,000,000—and this without invoking the
Low Countries, Scandinavia, or Finland and the three
Baltic states. If you wipe the entire Iberian Peninsula
out of the Italo-German ambit, but give to the Axis

Powers the allegiance of Poland, Central Europe, and the Balkan states down to (but excluding) Rumania and Greece, then Germany and Italy would have a massed strength of 200,000,000.

On the other hand, if Soviet Russia in Europe supported her Slav kinsmen in Poland, the Baltic states, Rumania, Bulgaria, and Yugoslavia, this Slav combination could muster on its own account 125,000,000 souls —and it would be a compact and continuous territory of Slavs, excluding only the Czecho-Slovaks.

If you take those small Powers which generally contrive to remain neutral, or have already announced a 'neutrality policy' towards the Great Powers' quarrels— the Scandinavian states, the two Low Countries, and Switzerland—and count their populations right out of the European ring, then the political or ideological divisions among Europe's peoples leave us with three main groups. First, there are the two Axis Powers, together with Czecho-Slovakia, Hungary, and a dubious kind of Fascist Spain: let us say anything from 145 to 170 million souls, according to General Franco's ability to control Spain for purposes of the Axis' policy. Secondly, we have Britain and France, with their 87 or 90 millions, according as we dare to include the Irish Free State. (We may add many more millions if we could rely on British and French communications overseas, but this question belongs to a later section of this book.) Finally, we have a vast tract of Slav country in Europe, from the Baltic as far as the Black, Adriatic, and Mediterranean Seas, from Berlin and Venice as far eastward as the Urals, with between 85,000,000 and

150,000,000 inhabitants—though this Slav *bloc* is as ideologically divided as the rest of the Continent, owing to the system under which 70,000,000 Russians-in-Europe are living. The Pan-Slav movement before the War has not been reborn in our own times largely because of the antipathies between the Slav peoples themselves—antipathies arising from the attitudes of the different Slav nations to the great Russian experiment. Of all the smaller Slav nations the Czecho-Slovakia of Masaryk and Beneš alone came into close sympathy and relationship with Russia, thereby incurring the hostility of the Nazi *régime*.

Before we leave the subject of population we may glance at the distribution of minorities in Europe after Munich.

The Jews must be left out of account here. If we examine all the countries east of the Rhine, Switzerland, and Italy we find that Poland and Rumania to-day possess the greatest minorities. Poland's population is now about 35,000,000 souls, of which only about 24,000,000, or two-thirds, have Polish as their mother tongue. There are now about 900,000 Germans in the country; over 100,000 Czechs; and about 8,000,000 Ukrainians (Little Russians, or Ruthenes), part of the 49,000,000-strong Ukrainian branch of the Slav family which stretches from south of Moscow and the banks of the Don to the Hungarian valleys of the Carpathians. There are also 40,000,000 Ukrainians in the U.S.S.R., 400,000 in Carpatho-Ukraine, and about 1,300,000 in Rumania.

Of Rumania's population of 20,000,000 only about

half—the core of the Rumanian people—is to be found in Old Rumania; the other half comprises 1,500,000 Hungarians in the Banat and Transylvania, 800,000 Germans, about 1,300,000 Ukrainians in Bessarabia and the Bukovina, about 500,000 Bulgars in and around the Dobrudja, Greeks, Turks, and the Jews. Whereas in Poland a strictly racial problem scarcely arises, save in the desire of the Polish Ukrainians to be independent, in Rumania there are minorities of all races and groups; and these minorities are disposed all round Rumania's frontiers. The true Rumanians, partly a Latinized stock, are mainly stuck in the middle of the country. Poland may dislike Russia, the Ukrainians may dislike both Russians and Poles, but all these peoples are of one racial stock. In Rumania, on the other hand, Rumans, Magyars, Germans, Bulgars, Jews, are all of different stock; and the Northern Slavs in Rumania, the Ukrainians and Russians, want to be separate from the Southern Slavs, the Bulgars, who claim return to, and are claimed by, Bulgaria, from which they were taken after the War. Both Poland and Rumania are as minority-ridden as the former Czecho-Slovakia, and infinitely more so than the new Czech and Slovak state. They have in them the seeds of disintegration, should an enemy foment domestic dissension among their peoples in order to destroy the unity of their states.

Almost as much of a jigsaw state is Jugoslavia. In the northern third of the kingdom are the Slovenes and Croats, Catholics, many of whom were citizens of Austria (Slovenes) or Hungary (Croats) before the War. In the middle are the various Serb tribes—Mohammedan, Catholic, and Orthodox. In the south are the Albanians, Montenegrins, Macedonians, and a few Bulgars. Slovenes and Croats, like Poles and Czecho-Slovaks, use the Latin alphabet; the rest, members of the Greek Orthodox, or Uniate, Church in the main, use the Cyrillic alphabet, like the Russians and Bulgars. Croats and Slovenes desire autonomy within the Kingdom. This is a potent source of contention between Belgrade and Zagreb; and in foreign policy, while the doughty Serbs as a people are strongly oriented towards the Czechs and Slovaks, they have no strong liking for Poles or Russians. On the other hand, their links with Bulgaria across their southern and eastern frontiers have been drawn closer in recent years, partly because they feel the dangers of either a German or Italo-German advance into the Balkan Peninsula. Against the Hungarians, of whom there are about 500,000 between Belgrade and the Jugoslav-Hungarian frontier, they have no pronounced feelings; and Jugoslav-Hungarian relations have been steadily improving.

Bulgaria, Greece, and Albania have a few minorities. Hungary has 500,000 Germans and — now — about 250,000 Slovaks, Ruthenes, and alien Jews.

On the whole, the dangers for the New Danubia, inherent in the kind of self-determination instituted at Munich, are to be sought in the national compositions of Poland, Rumania, and Jugoslavia. Any or all of these countries might be brought to internal dissolution through assiduous and judicious tampering with their different national groups by a Great Power. Moreover, such a Power could most successfully enlist others in the enterprise by promising neighbouring small Powers increments of territory and population culled from the disintegrating state. For example, Germany could easily enlist Hungarian aid in destroying Rumanian unity; for Germany could promise a return of the Transylvanian regions cut out of Hungary by the Treaty of Trianon. Germany could also enlist Polish aid by promising Poland a southern corridor to the Black Sea across the Ukrainian and Bessarabian lowlands, in return for the Polish Corridor in the north. Or, again, Germany could promise Bulgaria and Hungary together the return of Rumanian and Jugoslav territories, either or both, in exchange for aid against the two latter countries if these proved obstreperous.

It is a curious commentary on the present state of Pan-Slav feeling in Europe that Germany and Hungary, non-Slav countries, should be able to combine their claims on Slav countries to their mutual benefit, without arousing solidarity among the Slav nations. It is the more remarkable in that Poland and Rumania, the latter only partially a Slav country, stand to lose so much. But it would be dangerous even to-day to leave totalitarian Russia out of account. Adversity makes strange bed-fellows, and the ideological split between Russia and her Slav sister-nations may yet be healed. For example, if Germany constituted herself protector of all the Ukrainians in Poland, Russia, and Rumania, the repercussions on Poland, Rumania, and Russia might well be violent enough to produce once again a Pan-Slav solidarity. Such a contingency, however, can be over-estimated, for consider the case of the new Czecho-

Slovakia. Its population of under 10,000,000 is now completely controlled—politically, economically, and militarily—by Germany. Its policies are already turned to Germany's benefit, to the disadvantage of the Western Powers, of Poland and Rumania, and of other Slav nations. Its man-power stands at the disposal of Germany as much as its economic or armament resources. So great, indeed, has been the realignment of forces in the Danubian Basin since Munich that none can rely upon familiar or traditional allegiances.

(v) *Communications in the New Danubia*[1]

After the annexations of Austria and parts of Czecho-Slovakia Germany gained control of many vital arteries in the body politic and body economic of Central and South-eastern Europe. The mere control of these routes —by road, rail, and river—has always had a powerful influence on European history. It will now have a powerful influence upon Danubia's, and Europe's, destiny.

First, of course, Germany gained control of an immense strategic network of railways. Most of this network was centred on Vienna, the administrative, military, and economic heart of the old Habsburg Monarchy. In that Empire Bohemia, Moravia and Silesia, and Polish (or Ukrainian) Galicia into the bargain, were knit to Vienna by the railways which were built after the middle of last century for the purpose of developing trade with Central and South-eastern Europe. The chief industrial centres of Austria-Hungary lay in the Bohemian Sudeten-

[1] See map facing p. 176.

land, in what is now Polish Silesia round Kattowitz and Cracow, and finally round Vienna. Later the Hungarian capital, Budapest, began to develop a protected industry of its own.

All these industrial centres were knit together by double railway-lines, so that the Silesian district could supply Prague, Vienna, or Budapest direct, and any of the other three districts could supply its complementary districts by similar rail connexions. The railways from Budapest ran to Prague and the Sudetenland *via* Vienna; they ran to Silesia and Galicia through the Carpathians; and they ran down to Austrian Trieste and Hungarian Fiume, on the Adriatic, for their shipping. The main lines from Germany ran through Vienna and Budapest to Belgrade, Bucharest, Sofia, Athens, Stamboul, and Asia Minor. Another line came from Munich and Nuremburg, across Austria, through Croatia, to join at Belgrade. Yet a third line from Germany cut directly across Bohemia to Vienna, without touching Prague.

Finally, Vienna and Budapest were each linked with the Silesian mining and industrial region by independent lines across Moravia and Slovakia respectively. The historically important 'Moravian Gap' between the Bohemian Ore Mountains and the Carpathians, through which alone Russia and Poland (part of Russia before the War) could gain speedy access to the Danubian Basin, was crossed by two main sets of lines; and the whole 'gap' was in Austrian hands. After the War and the partition of Upper Silesia in 1921 Poland gained control of most of the Silesian industrial region. But she did not control the important railway junction of Bohumin. This vital junction had been made part of the new Czecho-Slovakia, when that country was carved out of the northern industrial and agricultural regions of Austria-Hungary.

By the end of 1938 the situation in Central Europe had been abruptly changed. Germany's State railways now ran directly to the Brenner and Carnic Passes, where they joined the main Italian lines from Italy's chief industrial region in the Lombardy Plain. They ran direct to the Hungarian and Jugoslav frontiers, thus controlling both main lines from Germany and Western Europe into the Danubian Basin and Balkans. The cessions of Czech territory to Germany, coupled with political and transport agreements with the new Czecho-Slovak Government at Prague, gave Germany control of the direct line across Bohemia from Saxony to Vienna. After March 1938 Germany controlled the main line through Austria to Vienna. The transport agreements between the German State railways and the new Czech state's remaining railway system permitted German use of all the Czecho-Slovak lines leading from Germany and Polish Silesia or Saxony in the north to the Austrian territories south of Czecho-Slovakia as curtailed after Munich. As far as rail communications were concerned, therefore, even the rump Czecho-Slovakia need not exist for Germany. Transit traffic was guaranteed at rates favourable to Germany; and the fact that Czecho-Slovakia's remaining railway system was cut across in so many places between the chief Czecho-Slovak towns by the weird shape of Germany's post-Munich frontiers made that Czecho-Slovak system dependent on German goodwill.

Moreover, since the frontiers between Czecho-Slovakia and Germany were finally fixed by direct agreement between Prague and Berlin (November 1938), the entire network of former Czech lines running both inside the old frontier and across it has passed into German hands. Thus Germany's boundaries now contain the important railways on both sides of the natural and historic mountain frontiers of former Czecho-Slovakia. The strategic importance of this acquisition cannot be over-estimated, since the new frontiers are indefensible by the new Czecho-Slovakia, even if it ever wanted to defend them against Germany. Accordingly German men and materials can henceforth be rushed into Central Europe by half a dozen separate double-track lines—from the Swiss and Italian frontiers, across the Jugoslav and Hungarian frontiers, through Bohemia, as far as Polish Silesia. It is not generally realized that since 1938 there is no country beyond Italy and Germany which can communicate by rail, road, or river with Western Europe without crossing a part of Germany or Italy.

Poland's position in the railway network of Central Europe is now of prime importance. It was one of the reasons which decided Colonel Beck, Poland's Foreign Minister, to carry out his long-matured plan to occupy Teschen-Bohumin as soon as Czecho-Slovakia's dismemberment in Germany's favour. This region contains a short but vital stretch of the line from Germany and the northern Czech line to Slovakia, Ruthenia, and Rumania. As Hungary was simultaneously securing the return of a long strip of South Slovakia and Ruthenia from Czecho-Slovakia Colonel Beck and his military colleagues, in order to assist that realization of the joint Polish-Hungarian plan to annex most of Slovakia and all Ruthenia, thus obtaining a common Polish-Hungarian frontier, decided that Poland must control the vital railway in the north, just as Hungary would have to control the southern line. Otherwise, German troops could be rapidly rushed the whole length of Slovakia-Ruthenia, separating Poland from Hungary, and menacing both Rumania and the Polish rear. In the event Polish troops occupied Teschen-Bohumin before Hungary had obtained any territory from Czecho-Slovakia under the Vienna award of the German and Italian arbitrators; and at the end of November 1938 Polish forces proceeded to occupy more Moravian-Silesian territory, together with the Czech rail junction at Cadca, before the due date for occupation. The possession of the Bohumin junction gives Poland control of all direct rail connexions between Czecho-Slovakia and German or Polish Silesia. It enables Poland to cut almost every rail connexion between three countries, and to prevent Germany from penetrating the Moravian Gap.

Consequently the only east-west railway between Prague, Bratislava, and Slovakia-Ruthenia fell under Polish or Hungarian control, as the railway connexions between Prague and Bratislava were already having to pass at two separate points through new German territories.

One or two curious details in this story of altered

communications are worthy of note. First, the lines which the Allied and Associated Powers in 1919 had agreed, in the name of self-determination, were vitally necessary to Czecho-Slovakia were taken away from her in 1938 and handed to Germany, Poland, and Hungary under the same guise of self-determination.

Secondly, Poland and Hungary now control the east-west railways through Moravia-Silesia, Slovakia, and Ruthenia to Rumania; Poland always controlled the eastward railways to Russia, except for the Baltic-coast route; Hungary controls the network round Budapest, leading to the Balkans; and Jugoslavia controls the Croatian-Slovenian bottleneck on the Orient Express route from the Balkans and Belgrade to Venice. Yet this entire Danubian network can be brought under German control by a simple operation. If the railway system of Hungary, the MÁV (Magyar State Railways), is forced to enter a preferential transport agreement with the German and Czech State railways—themselves already working in unison—then both the Jugoslav and the Polish flanks will be turned by German control of the Hungarian access to the railway system of the Danubian Basin and Balkans. Italian help in such a manœuvre could easily be obtained by Germany, owing to Italy's fears for the transit trade of Trieste and Fiume. This trade is dependent since the annexation of Austria on German (former Austrian) hinterland traffic across the Jugoslav bottleneck. Then if Italy and Germany proceeded to develop a common programme the control of both railways from Western Europe into the Balkans and Near East would be in Italo-German hands. Other aspects of this problem will be discussed later; but it is emphasized here that, despite the Polish and Hungarian acquisitions of vital Czecho-Slovak railways, neither Hungary and Poland together nor any other combination of smaller Powers beyond the Italian and German frontiers can now refuse, in the last resort, to enter a preferential rail-transport agreement with Germany, or Germany and Italy together. If you take the railway map of Europe and rule a line down from Danzig in the north, through Teschen-Bohumin (now Polish), Budapest, and Belgrade to the Adriatic in the south, you will find no single railway west of that line which does not quickly enter German or Italian territory.

In these days roads, especially planned motor-ways, are rapidly becoming more important than railways. If you need to transport easily handled goods, not bulky material like coal; if you need to rush an army from one province to another; if you want to do this at a high average speed—a motor-way, like the new motor-ways in Germany, is the best way. It is constructed with almost as much precision as a railway, so that gradients and turns are restricted to a minimum. An army transported at night along such a road can be more speedily moved than by train, for the capacity of trains is limited, and the capacity of the line is even more so. The new motor-roads can be marched along, motored along, or used as high-velocity superterranean canals for all kinds of goods.

That is, perhaps, why the Reichswehr immediately after Munich did not prevent by armed force the acquisition by Poland and Hungary of the east-west rail-

ways of Moravia-Silesia, Slovakia, and Ruthenia. It is
certainly why the Reich Government obtained from
the Czecho-Slovak Government in Prague in November
the cession of the 65-mile, 60-yard-wide corridor across
Moravia from north to south, to link Breslau, in
Prussian Silesia, with Vienna by a vast motor-way. If
one such corridor of German soil and property across
a nominally sovereign state, why not more? For
instance, with Italian goodwill, why not a new motor-
way across Jugoslavia's Croatian and Slovenian bottleneck to Trieste, Fiume, the Adriatic? That would only
be about 70–125 miles long. Another such road is
already in preparation from the Sudetenland to the
Ruthenian-Rumanian frontier. In this case several interesting points emerge. Such a road was long ago mooted
by the head of the great Czech shoemaking concern,
M. Jan Bata. It was then intended that the road should
form an alternative to the main trans-European highway through Austria and Hungary to the Balkans by
providing a northern route through Slovakia and
Ruthenia to Rumania. But during the two years before
the crisis of last autumn execution of M. Bata's pro-
posals was postponed in official Czech circles, owing to
the strategic use to which Germany might one day put
such a highway. Now the road is well on its way to
realization. It is reported that it is to be built by Czech
labour, but to German specifications; and its cost is to
be partly defrayed, according to reports from Prague,
out of the £10,000,000 'advance' to Czecho-Slovakia
by the British authorities after Munich. This road will
cross the new Breslau-Brünn-Vienna road-corridor

through Moravia; but when it runs into Slovakia, and more so in Ruthenia, difficulties will emerge. Hungary now holds the Slovak and Ruthene lowlands, and it is understood that German engineers have reported against the construction of highways or railways across the corrugated foothills of the Carpathians in Slovakia and Ruthenia as at present constituted.

Accordingly the German-Czech and German-Hungarian rail agreements, concluded in November 1938, assume greater importance. As Germany was able to obtain the right to equal treatment on Czech and Hungarian lines in territory that was Slovak-Ruthene or is still Czecho-Slovak, then why should not Germany be able to extract from Hungary the same right to own a strip of Slovak-Ruthene land, now Hungarian, in order to build yet another German highway across it to the Rumanian border? Indeed, there is no reason why German strategic roads should not now be begun throughout the entire Danube Basin, for that basin fell under Germany's control after Munich, and all the chief geographical vantage-points are now dominated by Germany.

Rumania and Poland, secure with their common frontier behind the great arc of the Carpathians and the Transylvanian Alps, might be able to wait a long time before becoming threatened by Germany's control of vital routes; but even in this case Poland has only the Moravian Gap as an outlet to Central Europe, Adriatic, or Mediterranean. That is now controlled by Germany and Czecho-Slovakia. The German highways into Hungary could be easily prolonged, by agreement with Jugoslavia, Bulgaria, and Greece, down the Danube, Morava, and Vardar valleys to Saloniki, whence the road would branch to Stamboul under the lee of the Rhodope Massif, and to Athens through Thessaly. Another highway has been mooted, branching from the one just described at Nish, the main rail junction in the Morava valley, where the Athens and Stamboul lines meet. This other highway would double the Stamboul railway across Bulgaria, down the Maritsa valley to Adrianople, Stamboul, and Asia Minor. It would be the highway equivalent of the Berlin-Bagdad railway, which played so intriguing a part in Central and South-east European politics and diplomacy during the ten years before 1914.

Finally, the trans-European motor-way, which is already in excellent condition through Hungary as far as Belgrade, would branch at the Jugoslav capital. One feeder road would run north-west to cross Croatia-Slovenia and join with the German highways coming down towards Trieste and the Adriatic, on what was once Austrian soil. Another branch would leave the former road in Bosniak Serbia, run up the Bosna river valley to Sarajevo, and then cross the Dalmatian Alpine range in Herzegovina to Mostar, and so down the short valley to the Adriatic.

Such a road network in the New Danubia would accomplish many things. It would greatly supplement and 'feed' the inadequate rail connexions in Central Europe and the Balkans. It would serve Germany's strategic purposes (of which more later) at the same time as it enabled Germany to assist all the Central and South-east European countries in a large, international public-works scheme. German engineers, technicians, and economists would collaborate with local experts in constructing what would virtually become a Pan-European highway network under German control. Each of the small Central and South-east European countries has a restricted budget, more restricted revenues, but plenty of idle peasants and labourers, plenty of undeveloped lands, plenty of local materials and resources. German, Czech, and Hungarian steel, Czech, Hungarian, and Jugoslav cement, petroleum products from Rumania —all these would be combined with German skill and local labour to create the most up-to-date system of land transport in Europe. Quantities of motor vehicles of all kinds would be required, thus creating a new demand for German products. Further, German experts would necessarily gain immensely valuable knowledge of the topographical and local conditions in all these countries. British engineers know that there is nothing like building a railway, a road, or a pipe-line in a foreign country for giving the best knowledge of the terrain, peoples, and communications.

We cannot leave the subject of communications without a backward glance at the map showing the altered political frontiers, the natural boundaries of various Danubian countries, and the geographical setting of the Old and New Danubia in the map of Europe entire.

Germany and Italy enjoy a sufficiency of road and rail connexions across their common frontier; but they are mainly confined to routes leading up from Venice and Trieste, through Villach and Salzburg, or else even farther to the east via Linz. Now that Germany has control of, and the right to use on equal terms, the direct Czech line from Vienna to Saxony through Pilsen, Italy and Germany proper have one more eastward connexion—through Linz or Vienna. But westward of the Venice-Villach-Salzburg connexion the former Austrian Federal Railways could provide only two connexions between Italy and Germany proper. One was the familiar pre-War Austrian line up from Italy to Trento and Balzano, over the Brenner Pass, and following the medieval trade-route all the way to Munich by Innsbruck and Kufstein. The other was equally dependent on the Brenner Pass line as far as Innsbruck, but then it went along the Arlberg line to Feldkirch, branched northward to Bregenz, and so linked up with the former German State Railways near Friedrichshafen and Lake Constance.

Consequently, the traffic between Germany and Italy to-day, everywhere west of the Villach-Venice connexion, is entirely dependent on the Trentino-Brenner-Innsbruck line—*unless*, and it is an important ' unless,' their mutual exchanges take place across Switzerland.

Switzerland offers Germany and Italy two extremely important rail connexions, equipped to deal with far more traffic in a day than is the Trentino-Brenner-Munich line. These are the Milan-Gotthard route *via* the Ticino salient to Arth-Goldau and Zürich, whence the line branches to Stuttgart, Ulm, Augsburg, or Munich; and, secondly, the Rome-Genoa line which joins the Lombardy line at Novara or Domodossola before entering the Simplon Tunnel to Berne, whence branches run to Basel or Zürich for Germany. There is an important switch-over formed by the diagonals of a quadrilateral with Domodossola, Novara, Luino, and Milan as its corners; and this enables Italian traffic to use the Genoa, Rome, or Lombardy-Venice trunk lines and enter Switzerland either by the Simplon or the Gotthard line. A separate line joins Bellinzona, in the Swiss Ticino, either to Novara or to Milan—the latter by a roundabout, alternative route.

The importance of these Swiss connexions becomes plain when we observe that, together with the Trentino-Brenner-Munich line (the closest link between Italy and Germany), they enable the two Axis Powers to exchange goods more speedily, and therefore in greater quantities, than can Germany to-day with Hungary and Jugoslavia combined.

But the position of the Swiss rail and road connexions is liable to make trouble for Switzerland either way, in the event of a war in which Italy and Germany were fighting on the same side, or in which one Axis Power wanted to help the other with war materials. Switzerland's integrity can only be guaranteed on condition that she herself does not prejudice it by allowing her territory or communications to be used for the transport of war materials, troops, etc., in favour of one belligerent, or set of belligerents, only. If in either of the events supposed above Switzerland were faced with a united demand from Italy and Germany for the use of the Simplon and Gotthard lines for war purposes, either Switzerland would have to take a stand on her neutral's rights and run the risk of a joint Italo-German military action against her, or she would have to give in to the demand, and become in consequence an occupied area, like war-time Belgium, with great doubts whether Germany would ever thenceforth evacuate German-speaking Switzerland, or Italy the long-coveted Ticino. In the latter case any enemies of Italy or Germany would be warranted in levying war on Switzerland too. In either case the risk that Switzerland, as we knew her hitherto, would disappear from the map of Europe is grave.

If Germany pocketed the German-speaking Swiss cantons while Italy pocketed the Italian-speaking cantons (Italy might also seize the Engadine, basing her claim on the Romansch—or Ladin-speaking Swiss element there, while Germany also occupied Liechtenstein), then Germany and Italy would extend their common frontier to include Berne and Basel—that is, including the Simplon and Gotthard lines. These hypotheses are to-day rendered possibilities by reason of the creation in March 1938 of the common Italo-German frontier, and because of the trend of Axis policy since Munich in September of that year. The importance of such considerations for France cannot be exaggerated, for they imply that France must reckon with Italo-German control of Switzerland to such a degree as will in effect achieve a continuous military—and perhaps economic—front against France from the Low Countries in the north right down to the Mediterranean.

Since Munich Hungary and Poland have not obtained a common frontier; but Hungary has secured almost complete control of the rail connexion between Czecho-Slovak Ruthenia and Russia proper, across the Rumanian Bukovina, by her acquisition of the east-west Slovak-Ruthene line. This, together with the Hungarians' control of all four pre-War lines from the Galician industrial region (Cracow-Lwów-Stanislawow) down into Hungary across Slovakia and Ruthenia, makes the Hungarian State Railways into an enormous strategic network.

If, following the agreements between Czech and Hungarian authorities and the German State Railways, the entire Czecho-Slovak and Hungarian networks are to function for German use on equal terms with their Czech and Hungarian users, the four Balkan Powers—Rumania, Bulgaria, Greece, and Jugoslavia—will find their rail, as well as their road, communications with the west under German control. Moreover, Poland, now vitally interested in Danubian trade and traffic, following her acquisition of the Bohumin railway junction and the Moravian Gap, is by the same token liable to become an objective of German plans. Very few people ever know anything about such recondite matters as rail tariffs—whether preferential, discriminatory, or otherwise—and, as the pre-War Habsburg Monarchy realized, preferential rail tariffs can be a potent influence on behalf of foreign policy. Doubtless Rumania, Greece, Bulgaria, and Jugoslavia can, at the worst, utilize the sea-routes through Ægean or Adriatic and Mediterranean; but, if cheap, these form a slow medium.

Though strictly outside the Danubian Basin, Poland's railway network deserves attention. The gradual Germanization, and in the last six years the Nazification, of the Free City of Danzig compelled Poland to develop the little port of Gdynia, on the Baltic, at the apex of the Polish Corridor between Germany proper and East

Prussia, as the important outlet of the Silesian-Gdynia railway. This line, financed mainly with French money and as recently as 1936, connects Poland's post-War industrial region in Upper Silesia—part of the Silesian-Galician territory of pre-War Austria—with the Baltic. It is her only connexion, by rail and sea, with the outside world independent of another country's territory. Moreover, the Polish industries in the 'strategic triangle' of Central Poland (of which more later) are linked with this Silesia-Gdynia railway, as well as with Warsaw and the Lwów-Stanislawow-Bukovina 'tail' of Poland, bordering on Rumania, by a very important second line. This leads from the Black Sea and Bucharest, in the south, to Warsaw through the 'triangle,' and to Danzig and Gdynia, in the north. From it radiate the lines leading to the Russian frontier, both in Rumania and Poland, and the line to Prague, Vienna, and Budapest. If ever the Polish Corridor were reoccupied by Germany, thus linking East Prussia and Danzig once more with the Fatherland, the entire network of Polish lines in the western half of the country would find itself in a huge salient, bounded in the west and north by Germany and in the south by a German-controlled Czecho-Slovakia as far as the Rumanian border. In that salient, useless except by dint of German goodwill, would be the Silesian industrial region, the connexions through the Moravian Gap with Danubia, and the entire Silesia-Gdynia line. Whether a Poland which was even anti-German could hope to protect Warsaw and the 'strategic triangle' south of the capital from an enveloping German and German-Czech movement is a question belonging properly to the strategic section of this book; but the importance of the Polish rail network in this context should not escape our notice, especially as it has a direct bearing upon the New Danubia. No German offensive towards " the undeveloped East " could unroll before Poland's recent acquisitions in the Moravian Gap have passed into German hands. In this task Czecho-Slovakia would be a valuable ally for Germany. Clearly the Polish and Baltic states' railway systems, connecting with Leningrad in the north, Moscow in the centre, and Kiev in the south, are as important on Germany's eastern flank as are the railway systems of Czecho-Slovakia and Hungary in Danubia proper.

The railways of Rumania, Bulgaria, Greece, and Turkey-in-Europe are few and rambling. Only those of Rumania have any immediate relevance to the New Danubia. Germany's retention of Ruthenia in the face of Polish and Hungarian desires brings, in effect, the German sphere of influence and communications to Rumania's back door. But this junction occurs in that remarkably difficult terrain on the farther side of the Carpathian arc known as the Bukovina. Here the only new railway is the line, not yet double-tracked, recently built by Czech and Rumanian co-operative effort as a link between Russia, Northern Rumania, and Czecho-Slovak Ruthenia. It is a line winding through deep Carpathian valleys, joining the Russo-Polish-Rumanian line below the junction of Cernauti (Czernowitz), and so running on to the Ukrainian network of the Soviet Union between Kiev and Odessa, on the Black Sea. It is doubtful if such a line can play any great strategic *rôle* either way.   More important in that part of Europe —indeed, for Rumania as a whole, with her central *massif* of Transylvania—are road and river connexions.

Perhaps the most important new geographical influence is that of the Danube itself.   It is a geographical influence on its own; but its new importance does not arise because of any violent change in its course, rather because of the violent change in the distribution of control over its waters.   The balance of power over the use of the Danube as a waterway, serving seven European Powers directly at the beginning of 1938, has now been changed so that it mainly serves Greater Germany; and the seven Powers have in effect now become only five—the Third Reich, Hungary, Jugoslavia, Rumania, and Bulgaria.   Austria, and the former Viennese headquarters of Danubian traffic control, are now inside Germany.   And Czecho-Slovakia, which until November 1938 had 170 miles of the Danube's northern bank, now merely touches the main stream at the point where Bratislava is almost surrounded by recent German and Hungarian acquisitions of territory.   Even then the rump Czecho-Slovakia's use of the river can only be on terms dictated by Germany or Hungary—or, to be precise, by both acting in concert.

Traffic on the Danube has always been mainly upstream, since the river flows away from industrial areas to agricultural.   Both before the War and after it supplied the needs of the countries in the Danubian Basin, chiefly their needs of raw materials, oil, timber, cereals, and bulk feeding-stuffs for cattle.   After the War, in common with the chief German rivers like the Rhine,

Oder, Niemen, and Elbe, the Danube was placed under an international *régime* guaranteeing equality of treatment for the landlocked states of the hinterland. In the case of the Danube, an International Danube Commission, with its headquarters at Vienna, was set up under the authority of the League of Nations; the internationalization of Germany's main rivers was provided for in an Article of the Versailles Treaty; and the pre-War Commission of the (Lower) Danube, with its headquarters at Galatz, was reorganized without Germany. While the traffic of the Danube has never been as voluminous as that of the Rhine or Elbe, the river has since the War developed as a feeder of raw materials to countries like Poland, Czecho-Slovakia, Hungary, and Jugoslavia. For Rumania and Bulgaria its importance as an outlet to the Black Sea has always been great. Goods coming upstream through Rumania-Bulgaria, Jugoslavia, Hungary-Czecho-Slovakia, and former Austria were transferred at various ports *en route*, put on rail or road, and conveyed to industrial regions as wide apart as Silesia-Galicia, Croatia-Slovenia, and Bavaria.

After the annexation of Austria in March 1938 Germany began to urge the Hungarian authorities to resign from the International Commission in the company of Germany and Italy. This demand was refused at the time, though it would have greatly complicated the position of former Czecho-Slovakia, since this country then shared a 170-mile length of Danube with Hungary, and if Germany and Hungary had repudiated the internationally guaranteed terms for the use of the Danube Czecho-Slovakia would have been caught between two fires. Nor could the International Commission have hoped to use force to sanction its writ against Germany or Hungary. Austria quitted the Commission in May. Italy declined to take part in its proceedings. Its headquarters were moved to Belgrade in June.

As it was, Germany contented herself with accelerating the widening and deepening of the Rhine-Main-Danube canal, thus preparing a deep waterway from the North to the Black Sea. She also acquired the Austrian commercial fleet on the Danube, amounting to 16 per cent. of all the Danube vessels. She began rapidly to build additions to the Austrian military flotilla in contravention of Austria's engagements to the Powers. And in all the Ripuarian states of the Danube her representatives began to forge ahead with offers of preferential freight rates on the German (formerly Austrian) cargo vessels, on the German stretch of the river, etc.

A German syndicate undertook to build the bypass canal from Cernavoda to Constanza, in Rumania, cutting through the neck of land around which the Danube meanders in its northward turn, and reaching the big Black Sea port in 50 miles instead of 250. Finally, when Czecho-Slovak territories were annexed by Germany and Hungary in the autumn of 1938 the Danube came fully under German-Hungarian control as far as the Jugoslav border. True, the Slovak capital, the part-German and part-Hungarian city of Bratislava, still had access to the Danube for a mile or two; but the new Hungarian acquisitions below Bratislava, and the new German acquisitions nearly all round it on both banks, deprived the new Czecho-Slovakia of any ability effectively to act as a conduit for upstream Danube traffic other than that bound for Germany. Till then Poland had imported not inconsiderable quantities of raw materials and fodder-stuffs through Slovakia. Now Poland is as dependent on German-Hungarian goodwill in this matter as the new Czecho-Slovakia.

More serious for all the New Danubia, if more striking in scope, is the German plan, immediately put into effect after the dismemberment of Czecho-Slovakia, for a new canal to link the river Oder and its canalized waters in German Silesia with the Danube, across the Opava-Bratislava gap created by the valleys of the Upper Oder and the March. This scheme, coupled with an older proposal to canalize and extend the Upper Elbe over the Iglau humpback into the valley of the March, when realized, will mean that the Third Reich will have no less than three separate waterways between the North or Baltic Seas and the Black Sea: (1) the Rhine-Main-Danube system; (2) the Elbe-Danube connexion; and (3) the Oder-March-Danube link. None of these will necessarily converge, or congest traffic, at any point. Again, as in the case of land transport, if the Reich controls the Czecho-Slovak and Hungarian waterways, a combined German-Czech-Magyar· transport system by road, rail, and river will both drain and feed, in compensatory directions, all the countries of Europe between Germany and Russia as far down as the Ægean Sea— Poland, Rumania, Bulgaria, and Jugoslavia. It must be remembered that, even for countries like Rumania, Bulgaria, Turkey, and Greece, which have outlets to the Black or Ægean Sea, the time taken by a tramp steamer to pursue its frequently interrupted journey through the Mediterranean to France, England, Scandinavia, the Low Countries, or Germany is very long compared with the financially more expensive, but chronologically more economical, use of the Danube valley's road, rail, and river communications. In proportion as the Third Reich contrives to systematize the German, Czech, and Hungarian transport systems—if no other—the 'pull' of the Reich on the whole of Central and South-east European trade will increase. If to such a system the transport networks of Italy, Jugoslavia, and Poland be added the argument becomes crushing. The Habsburg Monarchy was eminently successful in first creating, and then utilizing for political or strategic purposes, the 'pull' which its transport network exerted on various outlying countries.

To conclude this section we may take a rapid glance at the relief map of Europe beyond Germany. The Third Reich now controls Europe's most modern methods of communication across Europe's most ancient routes. If one end of such routes is not actually playing the part of a German bridgehead, then the Reich at least flanks the route for long enough to control it in a strategic sense. From the Low Countries up the Rhine to the Swiss peaks, along the whole Alpine range to Vienna, round the entire diamond-shaped mountain rim of what was once Czecho-Slovakia, up to the Baltic and down from the Alps, almost to within sight of the Adriatic, the Third Reich controls the passes, the valleys, the bridgeheads, the heights. Over the Bohemian, Moravian, and Austrian mountains the Reich has advanced, in less than six months, right into that saucer-like plain which is bounded only by the giant arc of the Carpathians, Balkans, and Dalmatian Alps. The countries inside the Danubian Basin—Czecho-Slovakia, Hungary, Jugoslavia, and part of Rumania—are pent up, devoid of natural defences, and too weak, singly or together, to improvise artificial defences against the Power which has burst in among them. Like the obverse of the Hunnish, Avar, Mongol, and Turkish waves which overswept these smaller nations in earlier centuries, a German wave has now started to sweep into the Danubian Basin, and on down what Napoleon called " the king of European rivers."

These accomplished facts imply a substantial change in what we have so long called the European balance of power. Control of contiguous territories, of populations, of communications, necessarily implies a strategic position, from which influence—either military or politico-economic backed by military power—can be exerted on other nations and on Europe itself. Before proceeding to examine the economic and political factors at work in the New Danubia, between the Third Reich and its neighbours, let us finish our survey of facts with a view of the strategic position of these countries. Such a view will provide a link between the alterations of frontiers, populations, and communications already noted, and the more ' human ' factors of economics and politics yet to be examined.

(vi) *Strategic Factors and the New Danubia*

The changes in the map of Europe during 1938, already discussed, are responsible for a fundamentally different lay-out of the European Powers' strategy and resources in the diplomatic arena.

What causes some nations to want the possessions, influence, prestige, or even inhabitants of other nations does not concern us here. We are forced to accept it as a datum. When we accept it, however, we have to face the policies, diplomacy, armaments, economic resources, with which the Powers conduct their relations, in an endeavour to achieve their aims—whether the latter be aggressive or retentive, active or passive. If, then, we try to assess the relative ability of this or that Power to attain its declared ends we are forced to take account of the theatre, the arena, the line-up of contesting Powers, the ' set-up ' of the contest in the uneasy peace-time that precedes the last arbiter between nations—war.

War, it was rightly held by Clausewitz, is to be viewed only as " a continuation of policy." Accordingly we have to review the expansionist policy of Nazi Germany after its successes in 1938, and to ask whether recent changes in Europe facilitate its " continuation."

It is dangerous to think that the times are now so abnormal that European affairs must be judged, and even conducted, by resort to random expedients. What we have seen between 1933 and 1938 in Europe, what is now in process of happening, is only part of an historical struggle between national forces in a crowded continent

—crowded not in the sense of being over-populated, but in the sense of harbouring tribes and nations with conflicting aims in a very narrow space. If those nations could only agree to sink their differences, to lower the walls of armaments and tariffs along their borders, to eliminate in effect all frontiers, and to bend their energies towards mutual understanding and co-operative effort, the result might well be that Europe—the most industrialized continent of the world—would find itself terribly under-populated. Indeed, it did so find itself in the relatively peaceful period between 1815 and 1870. As it is, the armament walls, like the tariff walls and other political or economic obstacles to international understanding, are by now so towering that the highest hope anyone nurses is only for an armistice, a halt in the process, not a return to relative political and economic and military disarmament. Consequently we must coldly assess the strategic factors in the new Central Europe, and see how far they help or hinder differing national policies. In short, what kind of theatre for war is the new Europe? To whose war-time advantage—and, therefore, to whose diplomatic advantage in the peace-before-war—have recent changes redounded?

Germany's acquisition of all the northern and western entries into the Danubian Basin must be viewed as part of the same policy which dared to remilitarize the Rhineland in March 1936. That policy was to immobilize the west and roll up the map of the east.

Germany's frontiers were not drastically altered after the Great War. The return of Alsace-Lorraine to France, the award of two small districts (Eupen and Malmédy) to Belgium, the loss of Memel, the fashioning of the Polish Corridor, and the Silesian settlement were the only changes to Germany in Europe. But the German nightmare—that of being beset simultaneously by the Slav hordes in the east and the French and British Empires in the west—was intensified for the future. To exorcise this grim spectre the Social Democratic Government of the German Weimar Republic and the new Soviet Union of Russian Republics concluded as early as 1922 the Rapallo Treaty, signed by Rathenau and Chicherin; and that treaty, despite Nazi Germany's supposed and proclaimed antipathy to Russia, has never been denounced. The ten-year Pact of Amity with Poland, signed in 1934, serves the same purpose; it was secured by Nazi Germany from Pilsudski after the French Government in 1933 had declined a Polish proposal for an immediate preventive war against the Nazi Party-State by France, Poland, and Czecho-Slovakia. The rôle of Czecho-Slovakia, as a French outpost and leader of the French-inspired and French-armed Little Entente trinity to the south-east of Germany, was suspect in Germany for the same natural reason.

Yet Germany, in the nature of things, was bound to seem encircled in Europe, for the very race doctrines of the Nazis themselves did not permit the dilution of good German Aryans by the so-called (equally Aryan) poor Slav stock. Slav nations surrounded Germany on the east, from Scandinavia and the Baltic down to Hungary; and once Austria had been annexed another Slav nation, Jugoslavia, had a common frontier with Germany. And in the west the British and French faced

Germany across a narrow trough formed by the two Low Countries or across the Rhine. Finally, after the annexation of Austria, Germany found her frontiers pushed down the Danube to a point where they met those of a non-European people, the Magyars. Accordingly, before Nazi Germany could feel secure from encirclement in a military sense, it was necessary that three things should be accomplished. First, the Rhineland must be rendered impregnable; secondly, the Czecho-Slovak bastion, a great natural stronghold, must be reduced without a war; and thirdly, thereafter, the remaining links between France and Germany's other neighbours, the Little Entente and Franco-Polish alliances, must be rendered null and void. If points one and two could be achieved point three would follow.

This threefold policy was bound up with two remoter German aims: first, the isolation of the remaining great Slav Power, Russia, to the east of Germany and Europe; and, secondly, the isolation of France and Britain in Western Europe. To secure the isolation of Russia from European councils was not difficult, since those directing British and French policy had no love or sympathy for the Russian *régime*. France alone in 1932–35 had tried to reinsure her Polish-Czech alliances by backing them with the Franco-Soviet Pact. But that was a Radical-Socialist and Socialist France. By the time that Germany dared France to oppose German troops reoccupying the Rhineland, in March 1936, France had drifted into a kind of internal political paralysis. The test of France's will and ability to bring Russia into action against Nazi Germany came over the German threat to France's other ally, Czecho-Slovakia. It was resolved by what happened before and at Munich. For good or ill, and whether she would have achieved anything effective in a possible war or not, Russia was utterly isolated from the west at Munich. The Russo-French, Czecho-Russian, and Czecho-French Pacts were in effect torn up. The new Czecho-Slovak Government was compelled by Germany to inform the Russian Government that Prague no longer considered the Czecho-Russian Pact to be binding. The German Foreign Minister, in Paris early in December to sign the German-French Pact guaranteeing mutual frontiers, extracted from M. Bonnet, the French Foreign Minister, so it is reported, an informal declaration that as long as M. Bonnet were Foreign Minister the Franco-Soviet Pact might be considered a dead letter.

Thus the Rhineland door was bolted and barred in the French face by the Siegfried Line, constructed since the Rhineland reoccupation of 1936, and Russia had been isolated from the rest of Europe by the German success at Munich. Further, at Munich the French had been isolated from Czecho-Slovakia; the Bohemian-Moravian bastion had not only been reduced, but its giant natural and man-made defences had been handed over to Germany to serve as German defences in future; and the French alliances with Poland and the remnant of the Little Entente were rendered derisory. A new Czecho-Slovakia arose, completely under German domination, as a kind of territorial and strategic outrider of the Third Reich, reaching down to Rumania and dividing Poland from Hungary. These two latter neighbours of the expanded Reich were made dependent on German goodwill. And, finally, Britain and France were isolated in Western Europe by the immeasurably increased solidarity of the Rome-Berlin Axis after Munich. (Discussion of the purely political and economic aspects of these statements must wait its turn for the moment. Here it is only our job to cast up a rough balance of strategic advantages, this way and that, in the new Europe.) If we take the foregoing as a rough approximation to the German Nazi view of Europe, especially after Munich, then the strategic lay-out of the European arena appears to be something like what now follows.

Germany now possesses a Reich boundary which is more secure than at any time in history. Neither Holland nor Belgium can attack her; the Franco-German frontier is a double line of fortifications, reckoned impassable in either direction. For the first time since the twelfth century an Italo-German combined dominion stretches from Denmark to Sicily, from France to Poland, Dalmatia, Hungary, the Carpathians. But whereas the Italo-German unitary Reich of the first Holy Roman Emperors was only loosely knit under the overlordship of a single man, the Rome-Berlin Axis functions as a diplomatic and military association, an alliance, a condominium. This condominium faces the two democratic Great Powers of the west, Britain and France. As a *bloc*, it is vulnerable in war on two counts only: (a) if its inadequate sea-power, compared with that of the British and French, results in a war of attrition from the word ' Go '—i.e., permits its foes to strangle it economically; and (*b*) if it finds itself, simultaneously or subsequently, threatened from the east or south-east of Europe—*i.e.*, finds itself caught between two fires.

Now, either of these dangers involves the entire Danubian Basin and its component countries. For (*a*) if Britain and France rely on a war of attrition, induced by the blockade of the Axis Powers which the Anglo-French Navies can impose, then the paramount question is, How long can Germany and Italy—for that matter, Germany alone, with a so-called neutral Italy—conduct a war on the supplies emanating from a Central and South-eastern Europe dominated by the Axis Powers? And (*b*) if Germany, or Germany and Italy, ever have to wage a war against the West a centrifugal movement among their eastern or south-eastern small neighbours—perhaps a new Pan-Slav movement under the leadership of the Russian colossus—would be doubly dangerous for Italy and Germany.

First, it would divide the Axis Powers' military efforts and resources for a war on two fronts; they would be caught in a pincers' movement. But, secondly, coupled with the hypothetical Anglo-French naval blockade, the revolt of the Slav and Magyar neighbours of the Reich would deprive Germany of her only alternative resources to those formerly imported from overseas. This would face Germany, during a war, with the need so to subdue and hold down her small eastern and south-eastern neighbours as to enable her to commandeer, or exploit, their resources. That is no easy task during a war.

Accordingly, if we coldly face the prospect of a general European war, the prospect of stalemate upon the ground along the Rhine frontier enhances the terrible importance of the New Danubia for the conduct of such a war.

But our assessment of forces must go much farther, once we have established even this elementary consideration. Leaving aside altogether the question whether such a European war may actually be *caused* by the expansion of Germany or Germany and Italy—a question which properly does not belong to the discussion of strategic problems—we can already see how immeasurably different the strategic factors will be in another European war, how changed they already are since the beginning of 1938.

A glance backward at Nazi foreign policy since 1933 gives us a hint of what Italo-German strategy in a general European war would be. German foreign policy, and German diplomacy which has helped to realize it, have both been employed to achieve a fourfold aim, now three-quarters achieved: (a) to occupy Italy elsewhere than in Danubia (Ethiopia, Spain, North Africa) and to give her all assistance; (b) to subjugate the Danubian countries whenever Italy was engaged up to the neck elsewhere (Austria, March 1938; Czecho-Slovakia, September 1938; Hungary, Poland, Jugoslavia, winter 1938–39; (c) to utilize Italy's resultant and complete dependence on Germany for the creation of a continuous strategic front, or axis, against Britain and France, confining them to the western tip of the Continent; (d) behind this front, rendered impassable, to weld all the East and South-east European states into a German instrument of economic and military conquest. Only (d) remains incomplete as yet; but the first three parts of the policy have been realized.

The question then arises: Will the Italo-German strategy be based on a ' drive ' to the west against Britain and France, or to the east against Poland, Rumania, and Russia?

The answer seems to be: On both drives.

Reasons for this are not far to seek. First, the *semblance* of an Italo-German threat to Britain and France (for example, with reference to colonies, Tunisia, Spain, and limitation of air forces) could be staged and utilized as a camouflage, to be generously renounced in Britain's and France's ' favour ' as a ' price paid by Germany and Italy for safeguarding peace in our time.' This would only be done, of course, to secure from Britain and France in return their permission to insulate them in the west while rolling up the map of Europe everywhere else. Secondly, a certain amount of trouble in the west is necessary to Italy and Germany to justify their rearmament burdens, to prove ' encirclement,' and to warrant their taking any action (for example, in Denmark, the Low Countries, Switzerland, Spain) to render the western Italo-German strategic front impregnable. Thirdly, though after the disappearance of Austria and the settlement at Munich there is scarcely any possibility of its occurrence, Italy must be prevented by Germany from ratting on the Rome-Berlin Axis—which can only be done by keeping Italy embroiled with France, since the British Government have for long, despite continuous disappointments, steadfastly tried to win Italy's favour. Fourthly, in order of their achievement by Italy and Germany, a western diplomatic 'drive,' stopping always just short of war, would be the best method of ensuring that the German economic and political control of Eastern and South-eastern Europe should be the prelude to the great eastern drive against Russia for the Ukraine and Near East. (Britain and France would be assured that the Axis Powers only wanted to eliminate Bolshevism from Europe.) Lastly, judicious manipulation now of the western drive and now of the eastern would enable Germany to grapple Italy to herself, insulate Britain and France, insulate Russia, and extort every passing advantage or piece of blackmail (Danzig, Memel, Danish Schleswig, Polish Silesia, the Corridor, and parts of Switzerland) into the bargain.

But when all these reasons have been studied there remains the most vital question: Are the two Axis Powers really partners in a war enterprise against France and Britain?

The development of German and Italian policy since 1935 suggests the reply. The Axis itself has in the last four years been forged piecemeal by Germany by cumbering Italy with commitments outside Central Europe. Italy has thus steadily lost all her advantages in the Danubian region, where once her dominion was scheduled to be set up. In the year 1938 alone Italy lost the shield of Austria, Czecho-Slovakia, and Hungary. She maintained a shadowy hold on Jugoslav and Bulgarian friendship only by reason of German tolerance and goodwill. Therewith Italian dependence on Germany for the crumbs from the rich British and French men's table, crumbs in the Eastern Mediterranean and

Africa, in Egypt or Morocco, Tunisia or Algeria, became absolute. Economically she is now more dependent on Germany than ever. Abandoned, Italy might wreck Germany's strategic scheme. But it is no less true that, driven back to British and French embraces, Italy would be the laggard in the class; she would have to sue for favours; and her enmity to Germany would expose her to the gravest direct dangers in a German attack on Venice, and indirect dangers like German control of Jugoslavia and the Adriatic. Accordingly Italy is compelled to stand with Germany.

But this makes Italian strategy merely a part of the entire European (even extra-European) strategy of the Nazis' Third Reich. And that is not *primarily* aimed at Britain and France. The *primary* objective of the Third Reich's foreign policy—and, therefore, of the strategy that may have to be set in operation to realize the policy —is the conquest, economic exploitation, and strategic organization of that vast European region which lies between the Right-wing Fascist Rome-Berlin Axis and the Left-wing Fascist state of Russia. That region is the Danubian Basin and its outlying flanks, the Balkans in the south and Poland in the north. Four years of German foreign policy and diplomacy, backed by German threats to employ rapidly multiplying armaments, were the prelude to the Austrian and Czecho-Slovak *pièces de résistance* in 1938. Now these are incorporated in the Reich's repertory, the unfolding of that strategic repertory can be better discerned. Possession of so much, so speedily acquired, so cheaply and peacefully gained, would clearly be prejudiced, gambled away, by a forthright and headlong challenge to Britain and France. Instead, the Reich has taken over the 'nibbling' policy of Clemenceau and Foch.

In the west diplomacy, arms, and threats will be used, in concert or alternately, by the two Axis Powers, to obtain such interim strategic advantages as can be extorted from Britain and France without risk either of a real war or else of a diplomatic defeat likely to endanger the domestic grip of the two Fascist *régimes*. Meanwhile, behind the Italo-German strategic axis (or front), the Third Reich will support Italy everywhere else but in Central Europe or the Balkans, simultaneously setting up the New Danubia and the new Eastern Europe for a German attack on the Ukraine with Polish help—or on Poland first, if the help is not ' offered.' This clash with Russia for the possession of all Eastern Europe—turning ' Asiatic ' Russia out of Europe " bag and baggage," as Gladstone wanted to turn out the " unspeakable Turk " —is said by Herr Hitler in *Mein Kampf* to be the sacred national duty of true Germans. Its sanctity will be rewarded, he says, by such material gains in the Ukraine and elsewhere as will make the German people " swim in plenty." " We can only look," says Herr Hitler, " to Russia."

Unfortunately, the original German text of *Mein Kampf* also prophesies, or advocates, the annihilation of France in a " final reckoning " *before* the Reich can build up and buttress its Danubian and eastern possessions.

Here we see the dilemma of Nazi diplomacy and strategy. How is France to be isolated from Britain and destroyed as a Power without a war? *Mein Kampf* was written in 1924. By the end of 1938, within a year, the New Danubia was under German domination, the French system of military alliances in Eastern and Central Europe was destroyed, the gateway was open towards Russia. The acquisition of the Danubian Basin was so brilliantly achieved by Germany as to throw even the oracular *Mein Kampf* into disorder; for by the end of 1938 the Third Reich and the Italian Empire could together exert combined threats on Britain and France, or, alternatively, woo first one and then the other, or each Axis Power could woo one democracy—for example, Italy wooing Britain, Germany wooing France. This possibility to pursue an ' insulation ' policy in the west was not foreseen in *Mein Kampf*. It permitted the east *versus* west dilemma in German strategy to be resolved —and the German General Staff's traditional fear of being beset simultaneously on east and west to be assuaged—by a simple solution: namely, a combination of offensives in east and west. In the west the offensive would be diplomatically a reality but militarily a bluff. In the east it would be a reality under both heads.

But—this was the great gain of 1938—at any moment the two Axis Powers might in future so arrange their policy that either the east or the west could be insulated strategically. That was never possible before Munich. It was thought by Herr Hitler to be impossible in 1924; otherwise he would never have reckoned with having to annihilate France, and hold off Britain at the same time, *before* building up his east, south-east, and Russian dominions in Europe. After Munich annihilation of

France was not even necessary for the realization of Nazi policy and strategy underlying the plans for the structure of the Third Reich. Insulation of the west alone would suffice.

But insulation still demanded a more impregnable strategic front in the west, an ever-expanding and ever more imposing array of armaments, lest the purely diplomatic offensive towards the Western Powers should, at any particular stage in the bluff or blackmail, unexpectedly provoke France or Britain to war. Such an outcome would, of course, be normally easy to prevent, since the unitary Italo-German diplomatic offensive to the west would be undertaken by one Axis Power against one Western Power, while the other Axis Power courted the other Western Power. Thus the two Western Great Powers might be kept divided; and, at the best, one Axis Power by soft words might actually wean one Western Power to put pressure on the other 'to safeguard the European peace'—that is, to sacrifice whatever either of the Axis Powers might at the moment be demanding from one isolated Western Power.

Italy could with soft words urge upon a friendly disposed British Government the advisability of compelling France to cede a strategic part of Tunisia to Italy, or to cede Alsace-Lorraine to Germany, or to do a colonial 'new deal' in favour of both Italy and Germany. Germany meanwhile could indignantly demand from Britain commercial and financial concessions or the return of colonies; otherwise all Europe beyond the eastern Italo-German borders should be accorded to Germany. At the same time the representatives of the Third Reich would be signing with those of France a renunciation of any claims against their existing European frontiers. As long as this game was kept up no issue ought to be raised *in the west* by the concerted Italo-German diplomacy that might bring Britain and France together in a war against the Axis Powers. And if Britain and France could be kept divided by such tactics all the easier would it be to bring under German organization the rest of Europe beyond the strategic front of the Axis. Such a peace would certainly have its victories; but only on condition that the Italo-German strategic front in the west were made impregnable. And that, in its turn, was virtually impossible as long as one danger, foreseen but not resolved in *Mein Kampf*, existed. That was lest the Western Powers should take Germany and Italy in the rear or on their eastern flanks. Munich settled the rear and the eastern flanks. What of the western front?

The German people were told by Herr Hitler in his closing speech to the Nuremberg Rally, on September 12, 1938, that " by the winter " the feverish activity of 480,000 German workers on the Rhineland fortifications (Siegfried Line) would be completed, and the German people would thenceforth be secure behind an impregnable barrier of steel and concrete. Such a barrier exists between France and Italy only in the form of the Alps. Between Germany and Italy in the west comes the narrow south-west to north-east valley of Switzerland; and we have already given reasons for thinking that any joint German-Italian offensive against the west would necessitate at least the Italo-German occupation (if not annexation) of German-speaking Swiss cantons and the Italian-speaking Ticino. The two Low Countries can be reckoned out of the picture—first, because both the German and French fortifications will be impassable: secondly, because *as long as Germany abides by the 1935 Anglo-German Naval Treaty and its limited categories of naval construction*, there is no point in extending the war at great cost to acquire naval bases on the Dutch or Belgian coast. As long as Germany accepts a 35-to-100 ratio between her Navy and the British she cannot face the mass of the British Fleet, even if that fleet has to reinforce the French in the Mediterranean. And if she cannot face the mass of the British Fleet her raiding and submarine campaigns can be carried on from the Baltic, Denmark, North German ports—perhaps, as we well remember from the Great War, from bases in neutral countries oversea. Consequently the Third Reich will be in a position to wage a desultory land war against France on the Rhine frontier and a harrying naval campaign on commercial shipping. But the important warlike effort is not even likely to be made on the Rhine frontiers of France at all. It is, for geographical reasons, most likely to be a combination of massed aerial bombardment of vital French and British centres, with massed land attacks on France through Switzerland and Italy.

Consider in such a hypothetical context the strategic lay-out of Western Europe after Munich.

The Rome-Berlin Axis was brought into play immediately after Munich to prevent Poland and Hungary from establishing a common frontier across Ruthenia.

Herr von Ribbentrop was dispatched to Rome at the end of October 1938, and Signor Mussolini and Count Ciano were compelled to support him at Vienna at the beginning of November, when Hungary was only handed Southern Ruthenia by the Italo-German 'arbitrators.' Germany thus retained the Ruthenian corridor separating Poland from Hungary. Therewith Germany prevented the Poles and Hungarians from beginning to construct a *bloc* of states round Germany which, though they might not fight against her, would in any case be better able in concert to extract terms from Germany, and perhaps even to prevent her from expanding over them singly. Thus from the Baltic states and Poland down to Rumania and Greece the Rome-Berlin Axis was in a position to threaten and control the strategic dispositions of any smaller Power. If Germany, Italy, and France in the west were entrenched behind unscalable barriers there were hardly any natural barriers left in Germany's path in the New Danubia or its eastern approaches.

The subjugation of Czecho-Slovakia at Munich released thirty-four divisions of the German Army for use elsewhere; to these 400,000 Reichswehr men must be added for the future all the field- and fortress-guns which the Munich Settlement compelled Czecho-Slovakia to leave to Germany. Their number is put at 1300; and their quality—they were manufactured by Skoda from Vitkovitze steel—is said to be above that of the Krupp material. Then there is the army of the new Czecho-Slovakia, incensed with the British and even more so with the French, detesting the Poles and Hungarians for their descent upon the carcass of the old Czecho-Slovakia, intent only upon loyal and grim co-operation with the Third Reich. That Czecho-Slovak army was mobilized to a strength of 400,000 fully trained men only six days before Munich, and within a week that figure would have been 650,000. It is not beyond the bounds of possibility—indeed, it is even probable—that the armed forces of the new Czecho-Slovakia, for reasons which must be discussed in the political section of this book, will be used in future to support the German Reichswehr in the Danubian Basin or the east. Almost as many German Reichswehr men will be set free to operate on other fronts. And if the new Czecho-Slovak army were not required by Germany to bring pressure on Poland, Hungary, or both, then *a fortiori* even more German troops would be released for action elsewhere. Let us, then, try to estimate how Germany and Italy could best help each other and dispose their forces within the framework of strategy now enlarged for them.

At this point it is impossible to consider merely Central Europe and the effects on Germany and Italy of the recent changes there. For, these changes being part and parcel of a unitary German, if not Italo-German, policy, the 'continuation' of such policy into the sphere of war leads us to recast our former ideas about air strength, naval strength, and land warfare. It also forces us to take account of a *combined* Italo-German strategy for all-European—indeed, for African and Asiatic—problems.

We need say little of the air arm, for it is established that neither Britain nor France could contemplate aerial attacks on their strategic centres in September 1938. Since then reports have placed the German Air Force at 12,000 machines in service trim, against the British 4000 and the French 1500. Italy is reported to have 2500–3500. And Germany's aircraft production in 1938 was placed at 650 per month to Britain's 250.

In the naval context the position of France in Europe and North Africa is important. The demolition at Munich of the entire post-War system of French alliances with Powers on the farther side of Germany, and the great increase in Italy's dependence on Germany after Munich, have combined to make the position of France exceedingly vulnerable to a joint Italo-German offensive. France would be as vulnerable in such an offensive, whether it were confined to policy and diplomacy or whether the two Axis Powers continued their policy into the sphere of war. Britain can only aid France indirectly—by bombarding Germany from the sea or the air, by attacking or blockading Italy, by transferring men or guns or munitions or aircraft to French bases for use by Frenchmen, or by immediately sending a small expeditionary force to the Continent—perhaps to Portugal, Spain, or Bordeaux. The small expeditionary force—it could scarcely be larger than 150,000 men, the size of the force that first left these shores in 1914, and might be less—would weigh lightly in the scale beside the kind of Italo-German threat which since Munich overhangs France. Not only is it the overpowering strength of the German and Italian Air Forces. It is also the complete turning of the tables on the French Army since 1936. Since Germany reoccupied the Rhineland and the Italians and Germans were tacitly permitted to control General Franco's forces in Spain France has been assiduously and successfully surrounded, in military terms. Now, instead of being Europe's chief offensive army, it is defensive. The importance of the changes in 1938 in Danubia is more to be gauged from the alterations they brought about in the position of *France* than from anything else. Since Munich the Spanish question, the query overhanging the future of Switzerland, the Italian claims (with German support) to Tunisia, have all showed up the beleaguerment of France.

In man-power Germany alone is preponderant over France; but not in the fighting quality of those men— a result of long training. The Reichswehr has only been able to count on general conscription since the beginning of 1935—that is, for four years. For the first three of these years the Reichswehr was recruited from a nation of 67,000,000 souls; for the last year from a nation of between 75 and 80 millions. The term of service was, on the average, one year; it is now shorter; so that since 1935 the Reichswehr has been enabled to raise the standing army to between 700,000 and 1,000,000 men. Of this number, however, only about 600,000 can be reckoned fully trained; the rest are in training; and over and above these there are the trained reserves, raising the mobilizable total to about 1,750,000 men. This is not a large figure for a nation of 80,000,000 population; but it must be remembered that Germany enjoys a reserve, now growing by about 200,000 a year, which has only been built up for four years. Every year that passes increases the reserve at her disposal.

Moreover, there are several para-military forces in Germany—Blackshirts (S.S.), Police, and Brownshirts (S.A.), together with Labour Service battalions—as well as the small Navy and the large Air Force. If these be included the total of armed and potential military services in the Reich would be about 2,500,000 in January of 1939. Of these, however—and this is a point where domestic matters impinge on strategy—at least 500,000 would be required for maintenance of civil administration and order at home—to secure communications, prevent civil disturbances or sabotage, guarantee the output of labour, etc. They would be like a police force. Consequently for the year 1939 Germany's man-power for strictly military purposes—that is, for offensive war in the various theatres chosen—would be about 1,750,000 men; it could scarcely be more, and might be less. Finally, the quality of training, equipment, etc., with which these men have been provided—whether in Army, Navy, or Air Force—is not, on the whole, as thorough or as good as that to which the French, Czecho-Slovak, or even British armed forces have been used in the last decade. This is not surprising in view of the breath-taking speed with which Nazi Germany has called forth her stupendous armaments. It has all been done in five years. France, Czecho-Slovakia, and Britain have had twenty.

France, on the other hand, has a standing army reputed to number some 500,000 men, of which 350,000 are fully trained. Here the comparison is made more difficult, because, owing to the decline in the birth-rate during the Great War, it became necessary three years ago for France to institute a retention of conscripts with the colours beyond the normal one-year term, extending to as much as two years. Even so, the two decades during which France's conscripts have been performing six months, or one year, or even two years, of service give France an immeasurably greater reserve on which to draw at full mobilization.

German experts have calculated that France can put into the field, within two weeks of mobilization decrees, fully as many men as Germany to-day (1939); and those men would be better trained, on the whole, than the rather rushed German conscripts. Of course, this would mean exactly double the strain on France, with only half of Germany's present population. Moreover, the French Navy is considerably larger than the German, which about balances the superiority of the German Air Force over that of France. Here it is sufficient to note that, since in modern warfare the offensive is said to need at least *four times* the man-power of the defensive in order to break through the curtain of fire-power which present-day weapons permit each man to unfold, neither France nor Germany is likely to be in a position to break through the other's defences. The outcome on the Rhine frontier, right down from the Belgian coast to the Gap de Belfort, which leads to the northern Swiss valley, is almost certain to be stalemate.

This stalemate in that theatre, however, only enhances the decisive importance of the other strategic factors.

In these the *rôle* of Italy is likely to be crucial. Now that Germany has no offensive to fear on her eastern and south-eastern flank some of the thirty-four divisions set free by the elimination of Czecho-Slovakia can be used to swing Italy and Jugoslavia into line with German policy. In this context the vulnerability of the Italian provinces of Istria (Trieste-Fiume), Venezia Giulia, and even Alto Adige must not be overlooked. Nor must the equal vulnerability of the northern Slovenian corridor in Jugoslavia be ignored, since it contains the pre-War Austrian towns of Marburg (Maribor) and Laibach (Ljubljana), and would give German Austria an outlet to the Adriatic.

Then there is the incomparably advantageous use to which both Germany and Italy (but only if they act together) can put General Franco and Spain, the Balearic and Canary and Fernando Po Islands, the Spanish zone of Morocco, and the bays in Spanish Rio Muni, in West Africa. This use can be primarily directed against France, but also against Britain. The Italian naval air bases in the Balearics threaten France's communications with North Africa, from which she is said to be able to recruit for her own army another 150,000 men (native soldiers). They threaten not only Marseilles, but also Corsica, the Riviera, and even Tunisia. The use of General Franco's aerodromes, built with German technicians' aid—or of all Spain, if General Franco is led to victory by Italian troops and German skill—will enable Germany and Italy to draw off to France's Pyrenean frontier a good proportion of the inadequate French Air Force, and some few divisions to safeguard Bordeaux and Toulouse. This Italo-German diversion in Spain will not be costly either to Germany or Italy; for in the long run Germany cannot hold out in Spain, nor can Italy, once a war with France has really begun. Still less would they be able to do so if Britain supported France with the British Navy and Air Force; and the possibility of a small British expeditionary force to Spain, *via* " Britain's oldest ally," Portugal (for whose defence Mr Chamberlain has pledged Britain to make war), should not be scouted.

On the other hand, though Germany and Italy in the long run lost everything in Spain, the diversion value of General Franco's bases, employed against France, would be considerable at the outset of war, progressively diminishing thereafter. If it be objected that General Franco himself declared during the Czecho-Slovak crisis that he would remain neutral if a war resulted, we need only recall that he received curt telegraphic orders from Rome and Berlin to attend to his own business, otherwise the Italo-German support for his continuously fruitless efforts would be peremptorily withdrawn, and he would ignominiously fail. Moreover, in December 1938 it was reported in many journals that both Italy and Germany were exploring the possibility of replacing General Franco himself by a Falangist more pronouncedly pro-German and pro-Italian, more amenable to " Axis policy."

It is at least clear that after Munich the diplomatic strategy of the two Axis Powers cast an ominous shadow across the military strategist's map of Western Europe; and for this the post-Munich collapse of Danubia beneath Germany's strength, taking a good deal of Italian independence with it, is in no small way responsible.

It is natural that, after combining to destroy France's eastern system of allegiances, Italy and Germany should turn on France, and not, let us say, on " mice and rats and such small deer" as Jugoslavia, Bulgaria, or Rumania. The reason for this—as, of course, for Italo-German aversion from an overt preparation for an onslaught on the Russian colossus—is that the altered situation in the whole of Central Europe permitted every advantage to be drawn from the insulated position of France and the French possessions. It was, therefore, to this end that Germany redoubled her efforts at the Nazification of Denmark and Switzerland in November of 1938.

The Danish deep-water harbours on the North Sea side (screened by Heligoland, now refortified in contravention of the Versailles Treaty) and on the Baltic lend themselves to German naval strategy. The key position of the northern and central Swiss valleys, acting as corridors between Germany and Italy as well as between both Axis Powers and France, is reported to form a major objective of Italo-German strategy. In the sphere of vital communications we have already shown their importance to the Axis. Finally, the abrupt Italian demonstrations at the beginning of December 1938 for " Nice, Corsica, and Tunisia " have their part in this Italo-German plan for an unbroken and unassailable front against the two western democratic Great Powers. If that front is primarily in process of construction against France, if it is intended to reinforce that front by the diversion value of a Falangist Spain, then what has been euphemistically termed in Italy " a regulation of the status of Italians in Tunisia " would, if peacefully extorted from France, set the seal on the division of Europe along the line of the Rome-Berlin Axis. It would, in fact, project the Axis into Africa. Behind a line from Denmark and Holland, down through Switzerland and Italy to Tunisia, the two Axis Powers might hope to be secure.

At this point the naval factor becomes important. Italy has a navy in which submarines and lighter modern craft up to cruisers both outnumber and outpace their French opposite numbers. But the Italian Navy has as yet no modern capital ships to compare with those of the French Fleet. Accordingly, as long as the Mediterranean Sea can be kept open along its whole length by the French and British Navies' superior gun-power, Italy is vulnerable. But at the time of the Italian attack on Ethiopia it was found that Italy had fortified the small island of Pantellaria, in the middle of the straits between Sicily and Tunisia. The straits are only seventy-five miles wide at their narrowest point. France has a vital strategic naval base at Bizerta, in Tunisia, just inside the western gateway to the straits, the use of which is accorded to Britain in case of need. The possession of a strip of Tunisia on the African mainland opposite Pantellaria and Sicily would enable Italy even to acquiesce in the French retention of the city of Tunis itself, or Bizerta, farther west. (Italy would not, of course, relax her efforts to obtain what her Roman crowds have demanded—the whole of Tunisia, with Tunis—but for the sake of securing European peace once more she might easily be persuaded to content herself with the aforesaid strip.) Then, with an Italian system of aerodromes, gun emplacements, and naval stations on the African mainland added to Libya, Italy would be able to render the passage of the straits so hazardous to capital ships of the French or British

Navy that, in effect, the Mediterranean would be divided into two separate lakes.

While Britain and France could still operate their navies in the Eastern Mediterranean, by using the long route round the Cape of Good Hope and up the east coast of Africa and the Suez Canal, it would be a lengthy and costly business. They might prefer to challenge the Italian forces at the outset, if need arose. In that case the toll on Italy would be heavy; but it would be very heavy, too, on the French and British Navies.

In any case, the Italian diplomatic onslaught on France and Tunisia at the end of 1938 made it quite clear that the two Axis Powers intended to employ their concerted efforts to cut off France, and by that token Britain, from Central and South-eastern Europe, as well as from the Eastern Mediterranean and Asia Minor, to which Danubia is the land gateway. Danubia and Tunisia—places far apart, but of equal strategic importance. One was given to Germany by Italian aid and acquiescence at Munich; the other was demanded (probably as a *quid pro quo*) by Germany's controlled Press for Italy the very day after Herr von Ribbentrop signed the Franco-German Pact renouncing mutual claims on the frontiers of France and Germany.

Indeed, the more one compares the post-Munich conduct of Italian and German diplomacy with the Munich Settlement, the more one is driven to the conclusion that (either at Munich, at Rome in October, or at Vienna in November) the German and Italian authorities decided to divide their commands—Germany securing Italian acquiescence in German control of Central and South-eastern Europe, Italy securing German support in Africa and Spain at France's expense. In this combined diplomacy success means great strategic advances over France and Britain for the future. It means the isolation of every European country lying beyond the Denmark-Tunisia line of the Italo-German front. It means that Germany's new dominions in the New Danubia as far as the Balkans (perhaps farther in future) can be safely exploited for the use, and the military strength, of the two Axis Powers. It is important to realize this aspect of the purely strategic lay-out of the new Europe, for, clearly, if Italy and Germany can simultaneously ensure their own self-sufficiency behind the Denmark-Tunisia front—that is, can snap their fingers at any Anglo-French naval blockade, and can ensure that war on land along that front is a stalemate, while war in the air across that front is at least not unfavourable to them—they can envisage not only a 'lightning-war' (*Blitzkrieg*), but also a war of some two years or more against Britain and France. They can do this, of course, only if other favourable conditions are granted them—for example, favourable domestic situations among their own peoples, the absence of revolt among their small neighbours behind the Italo-German front, the isolation of Russia, etc.

The kernel of the whole strategic nut can now be perceived. It is, as might be supposed, not a strategic problem at all. At the core it is compounded of economic, political, and even moral elements. Before we go on to examine each of these elements we do well to remember that the Nazis first raised the economic and 'civil' elements in strategy to their proper level of importance. While their experts, and the General Staff, drew up vast yet detailed strategic plans, they emphasized the dependence of such plans on the labourer's hours of work, the labourer's mobility between place and place, the importance of State regulation for key industries and industrialists—in short, the need of totalitarian politics and economics behind the machinery of a totalitarian war. Totalitarian diplomacy was used—as before, during, and after the Czecho-Slovak crisis—as a means to an end; and the end was a policy whose " continuation " into the sphere of war would cause the least upset in a totalitarian state. It is, therefore, the more surprising that in getting so far the Nazi and Fascist experts should have left so many important strategic factors out of account. It is to these that we must now turn before concluding this section.

We have mentioned that modern armaments, mechanization, etc., favour the defence rather than the attackers. That is mainly because of the vastly increased fire-power per man in present-day armies. We must now draw attention to the advantages enjoyed by France and Britain to-day. First, neither Britain nor France can be thought of as attackers of Germany or Italy. By this we do not mean that the French Army, or the British Navy or Air Force, will not assume the offensive in particular localities or circumstances. We mean that from the word ' go ' in the next European war Britain and France will have to fight on the assumption that the war has begun where in the Great War it had arrived only after more than two years—that is, at the point where a war of attrition, a totalitarian ' war of annihilation ' (Vernichtungskreig) sets in. That being so, and despite the terrible vulnerability of British and French centres of civil population under hostile aerial bombardment, Britain and France may be expected grimly to stand on the defensive, secure in their greater economic lasting power, compelling Germany and Italy (if Italy joins Germany) to spend their man-power, money, material resources, munitions, armaments, at the fourfold or fivefold rate required by a modern offensive.

Clearly, discussion of this particular factor must be postponed to the economic section; but it is important here to note that certain strategic implications at once emerge. For instance, Germany and Italy, no matter how invulnerable or how impassable their western front, will be forced to take the offensive. You hear to-day remarks like this: " Germany and Italy will try to play the Anglo-French game; they will wait for us to attack." That is completely to misconceive the nature of the totalitarian state's strategy, military apparatus, internal weaknesses, etc. The totalitarian state *must* take the offensive, for if it does not its social and economic weaknesses will rapidly lead its artificially disciplined unity to disintegrate, to vanish overnight. Its grip upon its own power and people can only be maintained under stresses. It is an unnatural hold. It relies on the hectic stress of an offensive war, a war that imperatively demands from every citizen, pro-*régime* or anti-*régime*, all of which his or her patriotism is capable—without time to gauge whether the *régime* is worthy of support or is achieving anything.

Again, war is but a continuation of policy; and if totalitarian foreign policy, conducted by totalitarian diplomacy, is only able to achieve success by the methods we have observed during the last four or five years, we cannot conclude that totalitarian war will be a passive, defensive, wearing-down kind of thing.

First and foremost, totalitarian states at war simply dare not allow their General Staffs and the peoples who form their massed armies time to "ruminate on the strange mutability of human affairs." The social, economic, and military effort required to raise and buttress the totalitarian state itself for a declaration of war leaves no reserve for a long war. And a war can only be quickly won by an offensive, which is steadily becoming more and more costly—that is, more liable to eat into such reserves of men and materials and munitions as can be mustered at the outbreak of war. Consequently there is in the nature of totalitarian strategy an obscure, but discomfiting, dilemma. Either the war must be won in a few months, a year at the most to-day, or it is lost before it begins. But if it is to be won quickly the *most* costly form of warfare must be launched from the outset by the states *least* fitted to stand its long duration. All the unproductive ' capital ' of armaments, squeezed out of the people's sacrifices, must be thrown into the scales from the word ' go.'

On this point it is perhaps worth remarking that German and Italian strategy has long been based on the assumption that (a) a *general* European war, or a war in the west, should at all costs be avoided by a diplomacy that threatens war merely in order to secure peaceful successes; and (b) that should a general European war break out, involving Italy along with Germany, it must be a war in which every kind of ' frightfulness ' must be employed at the outset in order to secure a rapid decision (not, as in the Great War, progressively as the war wound its way along). This second contingency is responsible for the Italo-German policy of building up enormous reserves of foodstuffs, industrial raw materials, armaments, munitions, armies, etc. If these resources, thrown into the scales of war at the outset, are sufficiently large they can be expected suddenly to overwhelm the combined resources of Britain and France by more than, let us say, the four-to-one ratio of superiority needed by the offensive in modern war. Britain and France, methodically and slowly laying out their industries and defence services to meet a war as long as the last, may, it is thought in totalitarian states, receive the rudest awakening of their entire history.

On the other hand, it should be known in Italy and Germany that the combined British and French Navies can afford cold-bloodedly to snap their fingers over their possessions in the Far East, can afford to cut losses in Asia, even perhaps in Asia Minor, the Near East, the Suez Canal, and the Eastern Mediterranean—*as long as* their warships can control the Atlantic, the Cape route to India and the Persian Gulf, and French and British home waters. As long as the British and French Navies can ensure the feeding and supplying of Anglo-French peoples and industries with the products of the Americas, the Dominions, Africa, and India, the vulnerability of Britain and France can be kept down to vulnerability from the air alone. The French may have to evacuate Savoy, lose Tunisia and Nice and even Corsica; Italy and Germany together may partition Switzerland, overrun

Holland and Belgium and Denmark and North Africa, dig themselves in (though this would be a ' suicide squadron's ' job!) in Spain, gain the military, political, and economic mastery of the New Danubia as far as Turkey and the Near East—but all this would not bring about what General Staff officers term a " decision." The war would go on, it can be argued, until scarcely a stone might be left standing in London or the Ruhr, in Paris and Lyon, or Milan and Munich; but as long as the 87,000,000 British and French in Europe, *plus* whomsoever they can draw and transport from overseas, can hold their fortified land fronts, feed their machines and men, and hem the two Axis Powers in by naval actions within the confines of the western front, the Baltic and Black Seas, and Russia—then, however frightful and barbaric be the cost of such a war, the Axis Powers could not win. They could not win because they could not impose a *military* decision. And all their totalitarian apparatus and warfare, heaped up more rapidly and at greater cost than that of their less prepared foes, might only serve to exhaust them more rapidly.

It is comprehensible from this strategic analysis that both the German and Italian *régimes* should fear, more than anything else, a general European war. If ever they provoke Britain and France actually to fight—however hard to imagine that may at present appear—their own initial advantages, so imposingly overbearing in so-called peace-time diplomacy, will begin to dwindle rapidly, while the initial disadvantages of the disorganized and enfeebled Anglo-French democracies will equally rapidly begin to be changed into growing advantages.

Of the frightful cost to civil populations, ethical and economic standards, human life and culture on both sides, we cannot take account here. But, viewed dispassionately as a scientific case, the strategic factor, apparently so favourable to the post-Munich overlords of all Europe beyond the Rhine and Alps, does not seem so in fact. It is a terrible comment on our civilization that we should have to conclude thus: in so-called peace, such as that through which we are at present passing, all the elements of the strategic lay-out in the new Europe redound to the advantage of Germany and Italy, either or both; for these two Powers employ those elements in a concerted diplomacy. That diplomacy succeeds by threatening a war. That war, however, if ever it came, would change the relative importance of the elements in the European strategic lay-out. They would progressively become less and less important in the conduct of war. More and more important, until decisively so, would the non-military, non-geographical elements in strategy become. Of these, the economic factor would probably prove to be paramount.

It is precisely at this juncture that the New Danubia once more emerges as a *deus ex machina* in the European drama, for both Italo-German diplomacy and the threat of military power behind it, which any considerable failure in their diplomacy may force them to fulfil, depend for their efficacy on the degree to which the Axis Powers can organize, exploit, and rely on the resources of Central and South-eastern Europe. The diplomacy and strategy of Italy and Germany have so far dovetailed. They have gained great advantages, and set the stage in the European theatre of warfare in a way apparently favourable to totalitarian actors. But the advantages and favours so gained can be used reliably only in peace-time policy. Once that policy is forced, however it be done, into its " continuation " of real war, the purely military advantages of Italo-German strategy seem to be endangered by other factors. To the consideration of these we now turn.

PART II
THE ECONOMIC FACTOR

(i) *Economic Changes in Danubia*

BESIDES the alterations to frontiers, populations, communications, and the strategic lay-out of Danubia in the year 1938, a great and fundamental economic revolution was accomplished within six months. Before we go on to estimate the effect of these economic changes in Europe as a whole, to assess the ultimate distribution of advantages and disadvantages so caused, we must describe the extent of the changes themselves.

The outstanding economic effects of the German annexation of Austria in March of 1938 occurred in the spheres of communications, raw materials, and labour supply.

With communications we have already dealt. It is sufficient to point out that on June 1, 1938, all the Austrian Federal Railways were placed under the control of the Reich Minister of Communications. Germany thus obtained a large supply of railway wagons, of which she was in need. On the other hand, the German State Railways had been forced by the prior needs of the Reich to neglect their proper maintenance and replacement works; accordingly the acquisition of the Austrian railways, themselves not so well equipped as the German, constituted a new charge on the greater Reich's resources.

But, besides giving Germany control of all the Austrian

railway network, the annexation of Austria gave her control over the outward and inward trade of Trieste, Italy's important Adriatic port. In 1931 23 per cent. of Trieste's seaborne trade for the world outside came from Austria; and in 1937 this figure had risen to 33 per cent. In 1931 22 per cent. of Trieste's inward seaborne trade was destined for Austria alone, and another 20 per cent. was consigned through Austria, on Austrian railways, to countries beyond. By 1937 the figures were 20 per cent. and 25 per cent. respectively. The leverage which this enabled Greater Germany to exert upon Italy can be gauged. Before the War, and to a less extent after it, Trieste—once Austrian, now Italian—served as the *entrepôt* and transit centre for Austria (including Czecho-Slovakia), Southern Poland (Galicia), and even Southern Germany. Its inward trade in coffee, colonial products, hides, fruits, metals, cotton, wool, and jute was so threatened by the annexation of Austria that a special meeting took place between German and Italian transport experts in May 1938; and when Herr Hitler was in Rome that month on his State visit to Signor Mussolini he is reported to have agreed to guarantee Trieste a minimum of transit trade on German account, amounting to slightly less than the total for the year 1935.

The reason why this year was chosen is that thereafter the effect of Signor Mussolini's Rome Protocols between Italy, Austria, and Hungary in 1934—an effect which weaned Austrian and Hungarian trade away from Germany in an attempt to block Germany's path to the south-east—began to become apparent in a large increase of Trieste's transit trade. An Italian office to increase this (primarily) Austrian traffic was set up in Vienna, in conjunction with the local Trieste Committee on Traffic (Comitato Triestino dei Traffici). After the passing of Austria Trieste, therefore, became dependent on Germany; and the North German Hansa cities—Bremen and Hamburg in particular—began to quote very low freight rates and dues in an effort to lure all Central European traffic away from Trieste.

As the distance from Vienna to Trieste is only 375 miles by rail, while from the North German ports it is 625 miles, the extent of the concessions in freight rates (both by rail and sea) necessary to lure away Trieste's normal transit traffic can easily be estimated. The Third Reich had either to shoulder an additional levy on the German people's national income to secure the North German traffic—in which case Italy's adherence to the Rome-Berlin Axis would be weakened—or else to annoy its own North German traders and shippers by keeping not-too-beloved Italian interests in Trieste happy. The acquisition of the former Czech industrial regions in September 1938 enhanced this difficulty for the Reich, for these regions had to a substantial extent drawn their raw materials from overseas through Trieste. Germany may now favour Trieste by annulling the German decree which abolished Czecho-Slovakia's preferential tariff on the old Austrian State Railways to Trieste. These preferences, regranted to Czecho-Slovakia, would aid Trieste. This peculiar problem is not yet settled, and the Trieste population is in consequence one of Signor Mussolini's most critical audiences.

As to raw materials, the important and strategic iron ore and steel-works of Austria fell to Germany. Of the iron-ore deposits those of the famous Alpin-Montan-Gesellschaft, estimated to contain 200,000,000 metric tons with a content of 30 per cent. iron, are the most valuable. The production in 1937 was 1,800,000 metric tons; of this, however, only about 300,000 was available over and above Austria's own needs, while Germany's needs of foreign iron ore in 1938 were placed at more than 20,000,000 metric tons. On the other hand, the acquisition of the Austrian steel industry, with an output in 1937 of 418,000 metric tons, was immediately capitalized by merging it with the big German Steel Union and the new Reichswerke " Hermann Goering " A.-G. The economies thus effected, in conjunction with new steel-works set up to work German low-grade ore under Field-marshal Goering's Four-year Plan, should enable the Reich to raise the output of former Austrian iron-mines and steel-works to double and treble their totals in 1937. In that case the integration of Austrian and German concerns will permit the Austrian armament and machinery works—for example, Mandl, Steyr —to concentrate on special work, orders and supplies of raw material being organized for the Reich's needs as a whole.

In this connexion the experts of the Four-year Plan have been enabled to carry out a far-reaching and efficient organization of the combined German and Austrian iron, steel, coal, armament, and engineering industries. In this scheme the former Austrian Alpan-Montan concern plays a leading *rôle*. In 1935 the company's accounts balanced for the first time since the financial and economic crisis broke out in Austria in 1931. The company, though its name derives from the peculiar iron-ore mountain, the deposits of which can virtually be worked at low cost on the surface, is also responsible for three-quarters of the total Austrian production of steel. Of its former capital of 3,000,000 shares, each of a denomination of 20 Austrian schillings, the German Steel Union held at the time of the annexation 1,600,000. Some indication of the value of this German holding can be gained from the report, during 1937, that the German Government estimated it at R.M. 30,000,000 or, at the real purchasing-power parity of exchange, about £1,500,000. The company had agreements for sharing in the European markets of international syndicates dealing in the following: raw steel sheets, sheet iron, sections, hoops, strips, tubes, rails. But, more important for Germany's trade drive to the south-east, the Alpin-Montan concern was a partner with the Hungarian (Rima-Murány, Gyösgyor) and Czech steel-works in the markets of Jugoslavia, Italy, and Albania, as well as the whole Central European territory.

But Austria brought to Germany other gains in the realm of raw materials. In the construction of light metal alloys for bearings and of aeroplanes magnesium is one of the most important elements. It is produced from the raw material magnesite, of which Austria was the world's largest producer. While former Germany had to import 178,756 metric tons of magnesite in 1937, the production in Austria for 1938 was estimated to be 180,000 tons, of which at least 165,000 tons would have been available for export. Thus, together with former Austria's consumption at home, Germany could count on covering all her own needs of magnesite; but, even more important, she could by the same token corner the entire Austrian output and prevent its reaching other countries—unless, of course, Germany herself sold it abroad for foreign exchange. In lead and zinc Austria had a small surplus; but, apart from these metals, the other big asset which Austria brought to Germany was timber.

Germany needed to import from foreign countries about 1,650,000 metric tons of round wood, 1,150,000 tons of sawn timber, and 3,100,000 tons of pulpwood in 1938. Austria could meet all her own needs and supply fully one-third of Germany's. Indeed, as soon as the German occupation was complete gangs of German labour-corps workers were sent to Austria, and a systematic stripping of Austria's great forests began. A forest, like a coal-mine, is a slowly wasting asset, unless no more trees are felled than come to maturity each year—which means that afforestation must, since trees grow slowly to maturity, be on a scale many times greater than the felling in any given year. Within less than a year since the annexation the felling programme in Austria has been many times greater than the afforestation programmes of the last decade put together.

In all cereals Austria's deficiencies merely increased those of Germany. Indeed, in wheat, maize, oats, rye, and barley Austria needs to import four times as much as Germany; so that the Greater Germany's dependence on cereal imports has notably increased. Austria's ability to dispose of her surplus milk, butter, and cheese will only help Germany very slightly, for the volume needed by Germany is so much greater. In all meat products, again, Austria's big deficiencies are added to Germany's and in one case, that of pig-meat, the import requirements of Austria are one-third greater than those of Germany. Germany's shortage of pig-meat has long been one of the most potent causes of grumbling among German consumers; and the other cause, shortage of eggs, is made worse by Austria's needs; so that the Reich Nutrition Board is faced with a more aggravated problem under this head.

In the case of raw materials for textiles, Austria's import requirements of raw cotton increase Germany's total needs by 16 per cent.; of wool, by 9 per cent.; of flax and hemp, by 13 per cent.; and in 1937 Germany's needs of all these imported textile fibres together amounted to no less than 360,000 metric tons. On the other hand, Austria needed to import yearly about 3,000,000 tons of coal and coke, which can now be met from Germany's annual surplus of about ten times that quantity. By the same token, however, Greater Germany cannot sell these 3,000,000 tons elsewhere for free foreign exchange to cover import requirements which Austria cannot meet. Moreover, though Germany gained Austria's output and surplus of electric current (she used to import electricity from both Austria and Switzerland), Austria's annual import need of about 400,000 metric tons of petroleum and ancillary products is now added to former Germany's annual requirement of about ten times as much—that is, 4,000,000 tons. Further, these are peace-time needs of oil. In war-time they might be expected to be multiplied by four or five.

Doubtless the costly process of substituting artificial for natural raw materials will now receive a fillip inside the Greater Germany. For instance, Austria had to import all her textile fibres, so that they accounted for 21 per cent. of her total imports, against which she exported finished textiles to the extent of 18 per cent. of all her exports. These exports went in substantial quantities to the other Central and South-east European states—that is, they competed with former German textiles. Now the Reich has organized the former Austrian textile industry in such a way as to utilize rayon, staple fibre, and other manufactured textile fibres, which can be made in Germany's large synthetic plants out of former Austria's surplus of wood-pulp (cellulose, etc.). Similarly, both Germany and former Austria needed to import rubber in large quantities. Despite Germany's progress in the development of " buna," the artificial substitute for rubber, Greater Germany's needs of rubber from abroad have been greatly increased; for " buna " is costly to produce in comparison with natural rubber, and Germany can only attempt to cover her own and Austria's needs either by taxing the entire German economy to the extent required to expand production of " buna," or else by forcing German exports into free-exchange markets, whence raw rubber may be bought in return. The same influences will be at work in the new Reich on production of substitutes (*Ersatz*) for metals and other compounds—for example, plastics.

Austria formerly used to import twice as much from the whole Danubian area as she imported from Germany. From the latter country she obtained more than 60 per cent. of her requirements of dyestuffs, electrical and other mechanical apparatus, metal products, paper, tools, and musical instruments. Germany accounted for more than 40 per cent. of Austria's imports of fertilizers (an important article of trade throughout Danubia), glassware, shoes and leather goods, pottery, ironmongery, motor-cars, chemicals, and furs. The annexation of Austria redirected former Austrian trade with Czecho-Slovakia, which before the War was the most industrialized section of the Habsburg Monarchy. More than 50 per cent. of Austrian imports of silk goods and pottery or porcelain came from former Czecho-Slovakia; and more than 30 per cent. of Austrian imports of coal, cotton yarns and textiles, wool yarns and textiles, minerals, glassware and metalware, came from Czech firms. In supplying Austria's needs of coal, minerals, glassware, pottery, and ironware Germany and Czecho-Slovakia formerly each covered more than 20 per cent. of Austria's imports under each head. Accordingly, after the annexation the redirection of Austrian trade to Germany dealt Czecho-Slovakia—especially the Austrian Sudetenland, with its export industries—a heavy blow. The articulation under the German Four-year Plan of both the former Austrian and former Czech (Sudeten) industries, with their needs of raw material, is consequently a serious economic problem for Germany. While it is true that the Czech industrial areas now inside Germany, together with all Austria, were complementary parts of the same pre-War economy—the Austro-Hungarian Monarchy—these industrial regions, both before the War and after it, have been developed for markets other than Germany. Among these Danubia and the Balkan States were very important. Now incorporated in the German system of controlled trade and currency, the formerly free export-import relations of Austria and the Sudetenland are superseded by the German system, which puts their local industries at a disadvantage. Moreover, both Austrian and Sudeten industrial workers were as efficient as, but were paid less than, German workers; and their standards of living were more modest. Accordingly the German system is having the effect of *raising* costs in Austria and the Sudetenland.

One of the effects of the annexation was to block Austria's access to Polish and Czech coal. Czech mines used to supply Austria with about 1,000,000 out of the 3,000,000 tons required, and Polish Silesia (also formerly part of pre-War Austria) used to supply another 1,000,000 tons. Germany at first broke off the contracts with Czech mines, substituting German coal for Austria's needs—Germany having a large export surplus of coal, as mentioned earlier. Moreover, Germany, in order to increase Czecho-Slovakia's economic difficulties and slightly to favour the German railways, prevented Polish coal from taking its traditional, normal, pre-War railway route along the pre-War Austrian line through Czecho-Slovakia from Silesia to Vienna. Instead, the reduced quantity of Polish coal which Germany permitted Austria to receive—partly as an admonitory gesture of 'goodwill' to Poland—had to be sent all the way round from Polish Silesia, through German Silesia, Saxony, and Bavaria. But then, within six months, Germany annexed large industrial portions of Czecho-Slovakia, and obtained a position of economic partnership in the running of the new Czecho-Slovakia, together with control of the Czech railway network. Consequently the boot was immediately taken off the Czech, and put on the Polish, foot. After 1938 Poland's acquisition of former Czech coal-mines in the Teschen-Bohumin area merely increased Poland's existing export surplus of coal, at the same time that the enlarged Third Reich obtained possession of the enormous coal deposits of former Czecho-Slovakia at Dux and Brüx.

Accordingly Germany's export surplus of coal was increased more than Poland's; and Poland found herself embarrassed by an enlargement of her coal deposits, coupled with a loss of almost all her former Austrian market. This economic discomfiture of Poland may be somewhat countered (though not to Poland's advantage) by the parallel German discovery that, after September of 1938, the large export textile industries of the Sudetenland were added to their old clients in Austria, forming an unwieldy and competitive textile industry alongside the old-established textile industries in Saxony, just over the former German-Czech border. The former Czecho-Slovak and Austrian textile industries were built up as complementary units in the pre-War Monarchy; they developed, even after the War, a large trade in yarns and finished goods, also in ancillary trades like dyeing and embroidery; and this combined Czecho-Slovak-

Austrian industry is now an embarrassing present to Germany. It increases the Third Reich's needs of the raw materials, competes with the established Saxon industry, and can only be turned to advantage by a big export offensive in foreign markets. That offensive has accordingly been started in Central and South-eastern Europe, as well as in Latin America, Scandinavia, and the Middle East.

In Austria's import trade Germany accounted in 1937 for 16 per cent., Czecho-Slovakia for 11 per cent., Hungary for 9 per cent., Jugoslavia for 8 per cent., Rumania for 6 per cent., Italy (despite the Rome Protocols of 1934) for only 5.5 per cent., Britain for less than 2.5 per cent., Poland for 1.5 per cent., and smaller shares went to France and Switzerland. All these countries must lose a certain amount of their sales to former Austria, since the combined German and former Czecho-Slovak suppliers will be enabled to meet most of Austria's needs. Even Austrian imports of meat and cattle from Hungary, Jugoslavia, and Poland were drastically curtailed after April 1938.

One of the most seriously affected clients of Austria is Italy, for Italy used to take between 30 and 50 per cent. of Austria's former exports of timber, all of which is now earmarked to cover Germany's pressing requirements. Consequently Italy is now more dependent on Germany economically than ever before. Whereas only 18 per cent. of Italy's foreign trade was taken by Austria and Germany in 1934, when Signor Mussolini concluded the Rome Protocols, that figure had risen by 1937 to 22 per cent.; and after 1938 Italy's requirements of former

Austrian timber, iron ore, steel, paper, etc., will have to rank after Germany's. The great political and strategic importance of this increased Italian economic dependence on Germany—a dependence still further increased by the position of Trieste and its transit trade—must not be overlooked when we come to discuss political trends and repercussions.

On the purely financial side Germany obtained in the vaults or portfolios of the former National Bank of Austria a welcome nest-egg of £18,000,000 in gold and foreign exchange. This came at a time when former Germany's exports had been suffering a substantial reduction because of the slump in world trade between 1937 and 1938. Her export surpluses had been converted into an import surplus of R.M. 33,000,000 in the month of January 1938, compared with an export surplus of R.M. 79,000,000 a year earlier; the import surplus for the first five months of 1938 was R.M. 85,000,000; and the stringency was so great that the Reich was being forced to do something which, however embarrassing to other countries, was not at all profitable to Germany —to buy on credit from the small countries of Central and South-east Europe and sell the same goods at *lower* prices, on world markets in order to ' raise the wind.'

This £18,000,000 was, therefore, a godsend; though that it was quickly swallowed up became apparent when, in negotiations in Berlin with Austria's creditors in May and June of 1938, it was found that there was no hope even of obtaining the gold reserve of the former Austrian National Bank, technically the guarantee of Austria's credit. The creditors pointed out that this reserve, coupled with Austria's foreign exchange holdings, exceeded the combined total (capital sum) of Austria's three outstanding international loans. But they discovered that the German authorities had been selling German-held foreign bonds to raise the wind, in terms of free foreign currency, to cover necessary imports even before the annexation of Austria. The £18,000,000, together with all the foreign securities and assets of all kinds formerly held by Austrian citizens, went into the maw of the Reich. It was a curious sidelight on Germany's acquisition of Austria, for at the time the currency and foreign exchange reserve of the Austrian National Bank was more than three times larger than that of Germany's Reichsbank, the published gold reserve of which was only £5,000,000.

Another acquisition by Germany in the financial sphere was the annual income from the 'invisible export' of Austria—her income in foreign countries from foreign tourists. Though the former Austrian tourist traffic fell away after the annexation, it still provides the Reich with a net income from abroad in free foreign exchange, without any commensurate need to import goods for tourists. This item was always the means by which Austria converted her normal surplus of imported merchandise into a surplus of exports (both 'visible,' like goods, and 'invisible,' like services to tourists); and out of her export surplus so achieved she used to pay the full annual services of her foreign indebtedness. Since the annexation and the Berlin negotiations on former Austrian debts Austria's payments of these services to her foreign creditors have been brought more into line with Germany's; that is, the enlarged Reich now has to find less foreign exchange under this head than the small independent Austria was able to do up till March 1938. Tourist traffic in Austria, therefore, brings in a net gain of foreign exchange to Germany.

Finally, there was a peculiar gain for Germany in the reservoir of 430,000 Austrian unemployed. In March 1938 there was an acute lack of skilled, and even of unskilled, labour in the Reich, mainly owing to the recent inauguration of conscription for the Reichswehr, coupled with the intensification of rearmament and strategic works. The Austrian unemployed were at once allocated for public works, roads, felling of trees, labour battalions on the Rhineland fortifications (especially during the 'rush' mobilization for the so-called autumn manœuvres in August 1938, before the Czecho-Slovak crisis), conscription for the Reichswehr itself, skilled work in German factories, rapid fortifications of Austria's frontier with Czecho-Slovakia, construction of new iron- and steel-works in Austria (for example, the branch of the Reichswerke " Hermann Goering " A.-G. near Linz), and even for agricultural work. This pool of Austrian unemployed was another godsend to Germany, as was shown when, in July and August 1938, special labour trains were run from Vienna to the Rhineland to accelerate the completion of the Siegfried Line there.

(ii) *The Czecho-Slovak Economy*

Before trying to assess the final economic effect of the annexation of Austria upon Germany's and other countries' positions we must take account of the equally far-reaching economic changes caused by the dismemberment of Czecho-Slovakia. These two small neighbours of the former Germany were neighbours, clients, and even complements of each other. Moreover, in the case of Czecho-Slovakia the economic changes are in a way more far-reaching than those in the case of Austria, for a rump Czecho-Slovakia has been left, under Greater Germany's economic domination. The precise economic *rôle* of the new state must therefore be gauged alongside the changes already accomplished. Finally, former Czecho-Slovakia's economic development and trade relations were different from those of Austria. Indeed, her national economic structure under the Peace Treaties was better founded and stabilized than that of post-War Austria, which was only two-thirds the size of Czecho-Slovakia, with half the population. Whereas Austria was a debtor on international account, Czecho-Slovakia was not. Whereas Austria was an enormous tadpole, with an over-populated, over-industrialized head at Vienna—containing more than a quarter of the country's entire population—dependent on imported foodstuffs for a large urban industrial community, Czecho-Slovakia was equally shaped like a tadpole, but Prague was only half the size of Vienna, and the national economy was equally balanced between industry and agriculture. Czecho-Slovakia was, indeed, an exporter of the highest qualities of manufactures and at the same time an exporter of foodstuffs—a rare combination in a modern state. Even the big industrial and banking concerns in Czecho-Slovakia were powerful in agriculture—and therefore, as we shall see, in the great Agrarian Party—through their politically acquired monopolies for spirits, wheat, rice, cattle, potatoes, and sugar.

But former Czecho-Slovakia's post-War problem, like that of Britain, was the unemployment which resulted from the curtailment and lagging of world trade. While, like Austria, Czecho-Slovakia could maintain agrarian profits and employment by raising high agricultural tariffs against the cheaper products from Poland or countries formerly part of the pre-War Monarchy—chiefly Hungary—she could not ensure that other countries would take her specialized exports. The Czecho-Slovak state, as we have seen, was given the ancient crownlands of Bohemia, with their mountain frontiers and natural communications, mainly on the advice of international experts. These pointed out that the post-War state would need the German industries and German workers established since the Middle Ages in the long, narrow valleys running down from the mountain frontier towards the ancient capital of Bohemia (Prague), and so eventually to Vienna. It is important to-day that we should bear in mind the development of these Bohemian industries within the lands of the Bohemian Crown, later to become Habsburg dominions. For their 'Germans' (*Sudetendeutsche*) were really Austrians from the end of the thirteenth century; and their export trade in many goods turned out by skilled labour went to serve the needs of the Central European peoples in the pre-War Monarchy, and beyond them into the Balkans.

These German-speaking districts along the Czech side of the Czech-German frontier began to develop overseas trade after 1880; their goods went to Hamburg, Bremen, or Danzig in greater quantities, and the old trade through Vienna to the Balkans, or to Trieste for the overseas countries, began to diminish. The difficulties of the post-War era in the export-industries of the Czech state were at their highest in the Sudetenland, because the German-speaking (formerly Austrian) factory-owners never believed in the durability of the Czecho-Slovak state; consequently they refused to undertake large pro-grammes of investment under Czech banking and financial control. On the other hand, the Czecho-Slovak Agrarian Party's shortsightedly selfish policy of high agricultural protectionism after the War—which benefited mainly the Slovak and Moravian agricultural estates—naturally deprived Poland, Hungary, and Jugoslavia of trade with Czecho-Slovakia. Accordingly Czech industries lost the export business with Hungary, Poland, and the Balkans which would have been the way to pay for imports of agricultural produce. Unemployment was, therefore, always high in the Sudeten districts, though certain markets (for example, Britain, U.S.A.) remained open to Czech goods. It was the slump in world trade after 1929 which paralysed the economic life of Czecho-Slovakia's German-speaking districts round her frontiers. For instance, in 1937—eight years after the slump began—there were still 166 textile factories closed in the Sudetenland.

The annexation of Austria, therefore, was a serious blow to Czecho-Slovakia, precisely because the textile and other export-industries situated in the Sudeten and other German-speaking regions had come to depend, to a large extent, on complementary trade between Austrian and Czecho-Slovak firms. It was natural that the two chief industrial areas of the pre-War Monarchy—that round Vienna and that of Bohemia-Moravia—should exchange the products of their special skill. In the textile industry, so important an export trade in the Czech Sudetenland, the business between Vienna and the Sudetenland was very great. All this was interrupted by the annexation of Austria, which came as the last crushing economic blow—not to Czecho-Slovakia as a whole, but principally to the formerly Austrian Sudetenland.

The dismemberment of Czecho-Slovakia effected at Munich and thereafter was more drastic from the economic standpoint than from any other. That Czecho-Slovakia should lose her ancient and natural frontiers, her costly fortifications, and over a million of her own people were painful facts. But that she should also have to lose every economic asset given her in 1919 to maintain her independence and economic balance, and this in the same name of self-determination as had been invoked to warrant the settlement of 1919, was indeed the irony of fate. In the former Czecho-Slovakia the ancient economic collaboration between Austro-Germans and Czechs was necessary and successful, just as it had been long before the War. The entire balanced economy of the post-War state, built up by unaided

Czech and Slovak efforts, savings, and skill, and developed during the world slump to a point of efficiency at which the state was not indebted, on balance, to the outside world, was torn asunder. Therewith a worse economic confusion was created than in 1919, for in 1919 at least the ancient economic unity of Bohemia-Moravia was preserved. In 1938 it was, for the first time in seven centuries, destroyed, German-speaking and Czech-speaking areas in one and the same big region being arbitrarily separated.

On the other hand, the very nature of the dismemberment in favour of Germany made it imperative, from the merely economic standpoint, that the new Czecho-Slovakia should enter into complete economic partnership with the Third Reich, working with, and within, the Reich system of trade and currency controls. We have already shown how far the alterations of frontiers have changed Czecho-Slovakia's communications with other countries. It remains to show the extent of the economic sacrifices sustained by the Czecho-Slovak state. Before we do this it may help us to describe the full extent of former Czecho-Slovakia's economic resources.

In 1937 Czecho-Slovakia was the sixth industrial state of Europe (excluding Russia). In the same year, and including all countries between Germany and Russia from the Baltic to the Ægean, Czecho-Slovakia produced 1,700,000 out of the 3,000,000 tons of pig-iron, and 2,300,000 out of the 4,700,000 tons of steel. Her armaments industry is greater than that of Italy, and in 1935 she was the largest exporter of armaments in the world.

All Czecho-Slovakia's heavy industries together produced more in 1937 than those of the eleven Eastern and Central European states (including Poland). It has been calculated that Czecho-Slovakia's output of armaments, steel, and fuel together amounts to more than half of the total war-power of the Eastern and Central European countries (excluding Germany). These heavy industries were the chief source of supply for all the needs of the Central and South-east European countries. Among Czecho-Slovakia's exports (amounting to £84,000,000) in 1937 iron manufactures accounted for 13 per cent., glassware for 6.6 per cent., cotton yarns and textiles for 5.7 per cent., woollen yarns and tissues for 5.6 per cent., copper and manufactures for 5.3 per cent., silk and silk tissues for 3.7 per cent., paper for 3.7 per cent. No other Central or South-east European country in 1937 even approached one-half of the value of Czecho-Slovakia's exports. The annual output of pit coal in former Czecho-Slovakia was about 17,000,000 tons, and of brown coal (lignite) about 18,000,000–20,000,000 tons. Coke, essential to steel-works, was produced to the extent of about 3,000,000 tons annually.

The cessions of territory to Germany, Poland, and Hungary have had the following results. The percentage of population now engaged in industry has fallen from 34.9 per cent. of the whole to 32.1 per cent.; and in agriculture it has risen from 34.6 per cent. to 37.6 per cent. According to figures published by the Statistical Office in Prague, the losses in Czecho-Slovakia's annual industrial production (as percentage of former annual output) are as follows:

	Per cent.		Per cent.
Stone industry	53.5	Hosiery	75.4
Fine ceramics	89.9	Laces, embroidery	74.5
China	98.0	Cellulose, cardboards	60.5
Sheet glass	100.0	Paper	62.8
Hollow and pressed glass	62.5	Bentwood furniture	57.1
Glass jewellery	69.6	Wooden articles	53.8
Heavy chemical industry	39.8	Musical instruments	86.2
Oil, fat, soap, and candles	62.7	Toys	63.0
Dyes	50.8	Fish preserves	66.4
Mineral waters	73.4	Vegetable preserves	57.4
Yarns	39.2	Hats	42.6
Haberdashery, buttons	86.7	Leather gloves	51.9
		Artificial flowers, feathers	92.4
		Umbrellas	48.0

In addition to Germany's acquisition of 26 per cent. of the former state's railway mileage, Germany and Poland together have taken lignite deposits accounting for 16 out of the 18,000,000–20,000,000 tons of annual output; pit-coal deposits accounting for 55 per cent. of the 17,000,000 tons of annual output; and the three beneficiaries (Germany, Hungary, Poland) have taken all former Czecho-Slovakia's graphite and zinc, 76 per cent. of her china clay (essential to her porcelain and china industries, which made Czecho-Slovakia the third largest exporter in the world of these goods), and 68 per cent. of her copper. Czecho-Slovakia is said to have lost 2317 industrial undertakings, of which (see the above table) 443 were engaged in the textile industry, 229 in glassware production, 260 in the jewellery trade, 85 in porcelain and ceramics, and 115 in the manufacture of musical instruments. These are all the leading export industries of the former state, and the new state's dependence on exports will therefore be diminished.

It is interesting at this stage to recall that after the War the Czecho-Slovak state inherited most of the industrial capacity of former Austria. She took all pre-War Austria's china and porcelain industry; over 90 per cent. of the sugar, glassware, and glove-making industries; over 75 per cent. of those turning out boots and shoes, chemicals, cottons, woollens, malt, and jute goods; and more than half of the industries producing alcohol of all kinds, metals and metal-ware, leather, and paper. It will be seen, from a comparison of these proportions with the losses recently sustained by Czecho-Slovakia, that the Third Reich has now obtained not only the bulk of pre-War Austria's industrial capacity (from Czecho-Slovakia), but also the whole of post-War Austria as well. Indeed, the very reason for giving the highly industrialized Sudeten regions to Czecho-Slovakia was that, historically and economically, they were the natural complement of the post-War state's largely agrarian economy. Now they have gone to an even more highly industrialized Third Reich.

Czecho-Slovakia has ceded to the Reich the valuable Joachimstal radium mine, which belonged to the state. (It was here that the Curies discovered radium in 1898.) She has lost the great Aussig chemical works, the spas of Marienbad and Karlsbad; and she has lost all the public services and municipal, as well as private, " installations " (to quote the Munich Agreement), which had to be left intact and handed over to Germany. Such include, for instance, the gas, electric, telephone, telegraph, sanitation, and tramway services; and public buildings as well as fortifications. On the other hand, the new state retains the famous Bata boot and shoe works at Zlin, the Skoda armament works at Pilsen (now within sight of the German frontier), the equally important and partly British-owned Vitkovitze steel-works near Moravska-Ostrava (now within five miles of the new Polish frontier), the Ceska-Moravska armament and steel-works, as well as the C.K.D., Brünn, and other such heavy engineering plants or arms factories. These, however, are virtually all situated within a stone's throw of German or Polish frontiers; their essential supplies of iron and fuel—whether coal, coke, or electricity—must now be imported from Germany or Poland; and all rail and road connexions between them must pass through foreign territory.

Another example of the new state's utter economic dependence on Germany is provided by the cession of 97 per cent. of Czecho-Slovakia's lignite to Germany and Poland; for on this brown coal depends most of the country's electricity supply, and now cities like Prague, Pilsen, and Brünn have to obtain either the 'neat' electricity from former Czech stations now in Germany or the lignite to make it.

Of the country's agricultural resources, Czecho-Slovakia ceded to Hungary the fertile regions of Southern Slovakia and Ruthenia—that is, the valleys running up to the Carpathians and down into the Danubian plain. She has had to cede half her forests to Germany, Poland, and Hungary; of these Germany obtains four-fifths. The capital value of these forests was estimated by the Czechs at £50,000,000 alone. The major portion of her lands on which hops, vines, maize, and tobacco were grown is lost to her, though she retains most of the sugar-beet fields. The latter will enhance her export capacity in prepared sugar; and the old Czecho-Slovakia was one of the chief sugar-exporting countries in the world. The former state supplied the highly industrialized Sudetenland and other regions now ceded with foodstuffs from her agricultural land; and it is interesting to note that the new Czecho-Slovakia has been compelled to agree to abolish customs duties on goods passing between the former Sudetenland and the new state.

Accordingly the new Czecho-Slovakia will be an important source of foodstuffs for the new regions of the Third Reich, at the same time as it can count on receiving its power, fuel, light, and industrial raw materials free of duty from territories which were formerly part of the state. In passing we may observe that in 1930 almost one-quarter of the German-speaking population of Czecho-Slovakia was engaged in agriculture or forestry. It was by no means a wholly industrial populace, and the proportion of Czechs engaged in agriculture in 1930 was only a little higher at 27.3 per cent. The major part of the remaining Germans and Czechs were engaged in industry. Consequently Germany acquires new agricultural estates and holdings in the former Czech territories. Of these less than one-half of the whole were in German hands in 1930; so that of the 800,000 Czechs taken into the Reich the majority are peasants and smallholders. The Germans have each, on the average, holdings of 5 hectares to 50 hectares; the Czechs have slightly smaller holdings. The importance both of these new agricultural lands and workers to Germany, and of the enhanced agricultural export capacity of the new Czecho-Slovakia across a frontier with no customs barrier, may be emphasized.

In the sphere of financial problems Czecho-Slovakia lost 40 per cent. of her sources of state revenue. This was caused not only by the loss of big agricultural and industrial assets in private hands, but also by the loss of forests, radium and lignite mines, power-stations, etc., formerly owned by the state. This is a larger proportionate loss than that of population, added to which is the fact that the Reich refuses to compensate Czecho-Slovakia for any assets taken over. That means that the new and truncated state has to assume the annual burden of the former state's internal indebtedness, with reduced taxable capacity and drastically curtailed national income. In the sphere of foreign indebtedness the new state is still saddled with former Czecho-Slovakia's small foreign debt, and the responsibility, shouldered by post-War Czecho-Slovakia, for meeting the services of 42 per cent. of the pre-War Austrian foreign debt, and on 16 per cent. of the pre-War Hungarian foreign debt. Equity demands that the Reich and Hungary, the chief beneficiaries after Munich, should at least take over responsibility for the bulk of this 42 per cent. and 16 per cent. of the pre-War Austrian and Hungarian foreign debts respectively. But it looks as though equity were likely to demand in vain.

As to finance, the Reich acquired some £30,000,000 of Czech currency and coin—almost one-third of the total circulation in the old republic—when it took over the Czecho-Slovak territories. German experts fixed an arbitrary exchange rate of 12 pfennig to the Czech crown (Kc.)—that is, making the Czech crown worth about 20 per cent. more in Reichsmarks than it was in any free foreign currency. This was an inducement to the Sudeten population, who obtained more Reichsmarks when handing over their Czech crowns than they would have done if they had bought, say, pounds sterling and transferred the pounds into marks. But this procedure resulted in a speedy conversion of all Czech crowns in circulation into marks—as it was devised to do; and the total sum of Czech crowns then collected by the German financial authorities became a vast fund of Czech currency, presentable to the Czech National Bank for redemption in gold or 'value receivable.' Of course, the National Bank could not hand out so much gold. For one thing, it did not possess it; it did not even possess gold and foreign assets to the total of one-third of its note circulation. Accordingly the Third Reich's experts in charge of the Four-year Plan secured a potent source of influence over the future of trade between the new state and the new Reich. For at any moment the Reich could demand redemption of a certain proportion of the existing coin and notes. Here, too, the Reich showed no disposition to compensate the dismembered country for so vicarious a liability.

Another financial problem arose from the many industrial undertakings in the ceded regions owned by Czech banks or private investors in Prague. Taking their stand on economic 'injustices' alleged by the Nazis to have been committed against the Sudetenland, the Reich authorities have so far refused to compensate such owners of former Czech enterprises now in the Reich. Instead, they are reported to be willing to set off these claims against the £30,000,000 of former Czech currency circulating in the annexed territories. This would mean that the Czech owners of property in the German regions would receive claims on the over-inflated liabilities (that is, banknotes) of the National Bank in a country practically half the size of former Czecho-Slovakia. This is a pretty problem for the financial authorities of the new state, and is likely to enhance their country's dependence on the Third Reich. It is a problem which must be added to another, and more disturbing, one: How can the new state maintain the stability of its currency independent of the German system of controlled currency, trade, and exchange?

At this point foreign trade enters the picture. The Czech crown was always a 'strong' currency, because Czecho-Slovakia's exports normally exceeded her imports (raw materials in the main) by about £10,000,000—sufficient not only to meet the services of her foreign debts, but also to pile up credit balances in free-exchange countries. Unfortunately for the new state, however, half of the former Czecho-Slovakia's exports were textiles and metal goods; and the new state has lost more than half of the textile industry, and perhaps a quarter of the combined metal industries. That will reduce its proceeds from exports.

On the other side of the account, while the new state will not have to find foreign exchange to pay for the raw materials for the Sudetenland's industries (Germany now incurs that burden), it will have to find almost as much, perhaps even more, in Reichsmarks to pay for imports of coal, lignite, electricity, iron ore, and other materials which it formerly possessed within its own territory. Thus its industrial export capacity is drastically curtailed (even though it exports more foodstuffs to regions now in the Reich) just when its needs of imported materials are being maintained. This will exercise a downward pressure on the Czech crown in terms of other currencies; and it is understood that this, in fact, was the real reason for the British Government's sudden generosity in offering the new state an 'advance' of £10,000,000 four days after Munich. It has been reported from Prague that the new state expects in a full year to have to meet a deficit on foreign trading account of about £10,000,000, instead of realizing the normal surplus of that amount. This means a turnover of £20,000,000 for a state half the size of the Czecho-Slovakia that could 'make' £10,000,000 out of a total of £90,000,000 of exports in a year. That is a big change.

It is hard to reconcile all the foregoing with the correspondence between Herr Hitler and the British Prime Minister at the end of September 1938. After Herr Hitler's second demands were put forward at Godesberg the British Prime Minister, in a letter dated September 26, pointed out to the Führer and Reichskanzler that Czecho-Slovakia's " national and economic independence would automatically disappear with the acceptance of the German plan." To this Herr Hitler replied on the next day that there could be " not the slightest question whatsoever of a check to the independence of Czecho-Slovakia. It is equally erroneous to talk of an economic rift. It is, on the contrary, a well-known fact that Czecho-Slovakia after the cession of the Sudeten German territory would constitute a healthier and more unified economic organism than before."

The only way in which that statement can bear scrutiny is if " Czecho-Slovakia after the cession " is healthier for, and more unified with, the Third Reich.

The new Czecho-Slovakia can only exist like a paralytic in an ' iron lung.' Its vital economic forces, its heart and arteries, its economic life-blood, can only function in so far as the Reich permits. Its remaining industries are dependent on raw materials that either must come from the territories which once belonged to Czecho-Slovakia or must be bought elsewhere with the proceeds of exports to the enlarged Reich. The new state has lost control not only of its internal communications, but also of the main entries into and exits from its territory. It cannot use the Moravian Gap into Poland and up to Gdynia without Polish permission, the Danube without German or Hungarian agreement, the Elbe or Oder without German consent, the railways to Hamburg, Vienna, Budapest, Trieste, or Rumanian cities and ports without German or Hungarian approval. The new motor-roads and canals which are to span its territory will either belong outright to, or be under the control of, Germany. Its trade and finances cannot be conducted without being dovetailed with the requirements of the Third Reich. These considerations acquire a special importance in view of reports that the financial authorities of the new state hope to secure loans amounting to £30,000,000 from Britain for the redressment of the country during the next two or three years. Britain took less than 10 per cent. of former Czecho-Slovakia's exports; Germany 20 per cent. Germany's power over the new state is much greater. So great is its economic dependence on Germany that a complete customs and currency union with the Reich would, from an objective standpoint, be more economically reasonable than the attempt to maintain a shadowy, nominal, unreal independence.

(iii) *The Reich's Economic Gains in 1938*

We must now try to assess the advantages and disadvantages to Germany of the territorial gains in March and September 1938. Clearly, what has already been described in detail gives some measure of these benefits and detriments, but the striking of a net balance one way or the other is a nice problem.

First, Germany has gained a total population of over 11,000,000 souls, in which, according to the statistics before each annexation, there were altogether about 525,000 industrial unemployed. These unemployed persons will be of great use to Germany in the acceleration of the armament and four-year plans. She has, in the second place, entirely covered her import requirements of graphite and antimony (from former Czecho-Slovakia), magnesite (from Austria), timber and pulpwood (from both). In metallurgical and engineering trades, in iron and steel production, Germany has gained control of a total output equivalent to about 15 per cent. of her own former production; but the former Czech portion of this gain depends on imports of iron ore, and increases the Reich's needs. Germany can now cover her needs of milk from Austria and of barley from Czecho-Slovakia.

On the other hand, Germany before the annexations had a surplus of pit coal and lignite (brown coal), which she now increases by the acquisition of former Czech mines and deposits. As to pit coal, Austria's needs will be covered by the exact amount of the gains from Czecho-Slovakia; so that Germany's increased lignite deposits alone will expand her surplus available for export or conversion to electricity. Yet she has also taken many important lignite-using power-stations from Czecho-Slovakia, as well as the hydro-electric stations of Austria which formerly sent current into Germany; so she is, on balance, almost cumbered with surplus electrical energy or the raw material thereof. The glass, china, porcelain, and textile industries of the Sudeten regions are a net addition to those of Saxony, as well as the complement to those of Austria; so that her capacity to produce is raised far above the needs of the new Reich, while, if she is to give all her new factories full employment, she is faced with imperative needs to import much bigger quantities of the relevant raw materials. Of these only china clay is supplied from Czecho-Slovakia. For instance, her import requirements of cotton, wool, flax, and hemp are now increased by nearly 50 per cent.—a prodigious increase which may mean a net addition of some £12,000,000 to Germany's import bill. And the overwhelming bulk of this increase must be bought with free foreign exchange.

Again, the annexations have brought Germany the *surplus* iron ore of Austria—only about 3 per cent. of her import needs—but if the Reich is to have an option on the output of the remaining heavy industries and armament factories of Czecho-Slovakia then the available Austrian ore will have to go thither. Thus the strategic Skoda, C.K.D., Ceska-Moravska, Brünn, and Vitkovitze steel and armament works, though they are all within a few miles of Germany's new frontiers, can only be kept running to capacity for purely German demand if Germany sees that they secure *more than twice* the former iron ore surplus of Austria. In effect, therefore, the Third Reich's import needs of iron ore (three times her own resources, and covered as to 40 per cent. from Sweden, 40 per cent. from Lorraine, and 10 per cent. from General Franco's Spanish territories) have been increased by the annexations. For petroleum, oils, pyrites, copper, nickel, rubber, coffee, tobacco, cattle, meat, and all cereals save barley and oats her need to import has been greatly increased. An interesting effect of both annexations is the doubling of the Reich's need of pigs and pig-meat. To her increased import requirements of the textile fibres already mentioned must be added an enhanced need of hides and skins, jute, bauxite (aluminium ore), and phosphates.

Thus the outstanding disadvantages to the Reich are her increased requirements of iron ore and textile fibres from abroad. Against these we must set the increase in her capacity to export finished textiles, metal-ware, glass, porcelain and china, cheap jewellery, gloves, coal, and sugar. But we cannot even yet proceed to strike our balance of advantage and disadvantage, for we must consider the *direction* of former Austrian and Czecho-Slovak exports, as well as the possibility—we might say probability—that the Third Reich will either deliberately or involuntarily assume responsibility for directing on broad lines the national economy of the new Czecho-Slovakia.

The direction of former Austria's foreign trade has already had to be altered to serve, primarily, German needs; and to that extent Germany has lost the latitude, which a large Austrian export trade would have given her, to secure free foreign exchange in payment for Austrian exports. Now that the Sudeten industries, competitive with German industries and complementary to Austrian undertakings, are added to the Reich, Germany will be forced to launch a widespread drive to secure foreign markets anywhere and everywhere. Without such a trade offensive she cannot possibly cover her enhanced import requirements over so extensive a range of raw materials.

On geographical, strategic, and economic grounds the Third Reich will assume responsibility for the distribution and allocation of the new Czecho-Slovakia's imports and exports. Far from being " a healthier and more unified economic organism than before," the new Czecho-Slovakia can only be of strategic and economic benefit to the Reich if the Reich, in its turn, takes over the burden of supplying it with the necessary materials from 'approved' quarters. In other words, the new state must be—if not nominally, then in effect—integrated with the economic system of the Reich, as it is already integrated in a remarkable and unprecedented fashion with the Reich's system of communications.

Of course, the authorities in charge of the Four-year Plan will not go out of their way to interrupt the new Czecho-Slovakia's trade connexions with foreign countries—especially those countries from which Czecho-Slovak exports can secure free foreign exchange. Indeed, the German authorities will do all in their power to encourage foreign countries to take the most charitable and generous view of unhappy Czecho-Slovakia's plight —in other words, to buy Czecho-Slovak goods, to invest money there (if possible), and generally to behave in economic terms as if the new state really was possessed of complete independence and sovereignty. But meanwhile the markets of industries in both the new Sudeten industrial region of the Reich and rump Czecho-Slovakia are much the same. The German and Czech industries are likely to be in competition in Danubia, the Balkans, and other countries. Consequently the integration, or close organization, of Czech and new German export industries becomes imperative. And as this dovetailing process goes ahead, so will the Reich find itself faced with more and more redundant export capacity, greater needs of imported raw materials if the industries are all to be kept going, or else the necessity completely to eliminate certain factories in the Sudetenland and Czecho-Slovakia in favour of industries newly to be established. Ultimately, therefore, the Reich faces an increased need of liquid capital for new investments before it can hope to draw trading or financial advantages from its recent acquisitions.

These are all disadvantages occasioned by the need for drastic reorganization of Germany's, Austria's, and Czecho-Slovakia's import and export trade. There are, however, ultimate advantages of a very high order to be secured by the Reich and the new Czecho-Slovakia, working together, if German reorganization is successful. For example, the recent annexations have greatly increased the Reich's 'pull' on the resources of all East and South-east European countries—indeed, on Italy as well. We need only cite the armament and engineering industries of Czecho-Slovakia, which supplied nearly all these countries with their requirements; the Austrian import market for Hungarian cereals; the Austrian and Czecho-Slovak markets for Greek and Bulgarian tobacco; and the Austro-Czecho-Slovak requirements of Rumanian oil. If we add this kind of economic 'pull' to the influence exercisable by the Reich through its greatly extended network of vital communications, and then add the former Germany's dominant economic power in all Central and South-eastern Europe, the possibility that the Reich's experts will organize their recently acquired economic assets for a trade offensive is hardly open to doubt.

Thus, on balance, Germany has shouldered in quick succession two formidable economic problems. For an indefinable interim period they may be a cumbersome burden. But in the long run, which may not prove to be so very long, the burden will probably turn out to be a load of net advantages. To achieve this fortunate result, however, the Reich will need to redistribute its import and export trade, to find much new liquid capital for investments, and to drive its exports into foreign markets at almost any cost. This preparatory procedure is the most costly, and without it the new economic accessions may prove embarrassing encumbrances. Whether the expanded Reich will, in fact, be able to accomplish the ends for which it has recently acquired substantial new means is a question demanding a separate stage in our inquiry. For though the Reich has now obtained control of all approaches to, and communications in, the New Danubia, though it has rapidly extended and tightened its grip on the requirements and resources of the Danubian countries—it has, ever since its foundation in 1933, encountered its most serious obstacles not, as its spokesmen aver, in the economic field of a hostile outside world, but in the field of its own domestic economy. The difficulties which the Reich has met in conducting its foreign trade have been in the main difficulties of its own making. Its recent territorial and economic acquisitions may well enhance these problems at home, in the Reich itself. And if those domestic economic problems are not solved, then the Reich's ability to organize a lasting and efficient economic development of the New Danubia for German ends will be doubtful. It may not even exist. We therefore go on to examine the *rôle* and influence of the Reich in meeting the needs, and utilizing the resources, of the Danubian countries.

(iv) *Germany's Sinews of War*

In five years the Third Reich has built up the biggest
land army on the Continent (excluding that of Russia),
the largest air force, a vast network of modern strategic
highways, the largest economic war-machine, and a navy
large enough to dominate the Baltic and, perhaps, to
ward off naval assaults upon German harbours either in
the Baltic or North Sea. Moreover, the Nazi architects
of the Reich have reduced ' statistical ' unemployment
from 6,000,000, out of a population of some 65,500,000,
in 1932 to about 300,000, out of a population of
80,000,000, at the end of 1938. The word ' statistical '
must be used, since in the meantime the number of
men taken off the labour market and employed by the
Nazi Party-State as conscripts in the Reichswehr, in the
Blackshirt divisions, Brownshirt organizations (S.A.),
Secret Police, labour camps, and concentration camps
cannot be less than 3,000,000. In the same period Germany's output of iron and steel in 1938 was half as
much again as it was in 1929, compared with an increase
of a mere 8 per cent. in the British output; and her
industrial production as a whole was running in 1938 at
about a quarter more than in 1929, while British industrial production in the same period showed an increase
of only 8 per cent.

How was this achieved? And can the now greatly
expanded Reich go on to the highest pitch of economic
effort—that of war?

The easiest way to answer these searching economic
questions is to describe how the Nazi authorities set

about the realization of their aims. These aims were primarily political and strategic. The means to achieve them were economic. The dictatorship claimed and exercised power over all aspects of individual and communal life in Germany. That was both a political means and a political end. But the Party programme went beyond that. The authoritarian Right-wing Party-State was to aim at diplomatic and strategic successes in the foreign field.

To achieve this economic strength was necessary, but Germany in 1933 was woefully weak. The foreign loans (from American, British, French, Dutch, Swiss, and Swedish lenders) which had poured into Republican Germany from the post-inflation settlement and Dawes Loan of 1924 until the Young Loan of 1930, ostensibly to enable Germany to pay reparations, ceased to trickle in 1930. Only about two-thirds of the German borrowings were in fact used to equip the German industries engaged in payment of reparations-in-kind or in export trades to gain the foreign exchange to pay reparations and loan services. The rest was used to modernize and embellish the republic's railways, communications, public services, municipalities, docks and harbours, air-ports, etc. In addition to these long-term loans, German banks and enterprises borrowed (and unwise foreign authorities lent) between 1928 and 1931 on short term—for example, for three months, renewable for another three months, and so on—about £650,000,000. When the financial crisis broke out in Austria in May 1931, and the Hoover Moratorium on international political indebtedness was hurriedly declared, the short-term creditors in a panic removed some £150,000,000 from Germany; but the rest had to remain, with their enforced agreement, under what was called a 'Standstill Agreement.' Under this no repayment of principal of these short-term loans was required for the moment, but the interest was paid and transferred. As the financial crisis became more intense in 1932 the Governments of Chancellors Brüning, Von Papen, and Von Schleicher—the last Governments of the Weimar Republic—were driven to demand the 'blocking' of all foreign requests for transfer of foreign-owned assets from Germany, and to require reductions in interest, in order to maintain the value of the Reichsmark. The slump in world trade had hit Germany as hard as it had hit Great Britain; and Britain had depreciated the pound sterling in September 1931 under pressure of demands for the return of foreign-owned funds in London. There was nothing peculiar in the Weimar Republic's economic position in 1932. The Reichsmark was imperilled by a slump in the vital German export trade, coupled with the necessity to maintain imports; and this was aggravated by a sudden conjuncture of foreign demands for the return of funds lent to Germany, when the going was good, in earlier years.

But with the advent of Herr Hitler's Nazi Party to power at the end of January 1933 the economic situation of Germany underwent something like a revolution. First, the Nazi Party had always made " the overthrow of the tyranny of interest " a cardinal feature in its economic programme. Dr Schacht was enabled, with Nazi support, to 'block' virtually all transfers abroad of the services on Germany's long-term debts (the Dawes and Young Loans were excluded), and to renew from year to year, right up to the present, the Standstill Agreements. Accordingly the value of assets held in Germany by foreigners suffered sharp reductions, for the prospect of ever retrieving the sum actually lent became ever smaller. The German experts invoked the 'transfer problem' in justification, pointing out, with some warranty, that unless Germany could secure and maintain a large export surplus, over and above her paramount need of imports, she could not possibly secure the free foreign exchange wherewith to repay the principal of former short-term debt, the annually agreed services of both short- and long-term debts, and the annual repayments of principal for amortization (redemption) of the long-term debt. But an adequate export surplus was never realized, since the Reich increased its imports of strategic materials to a point at which exports scarcely sufficed to pay for them. Moreover, reparations were virtually abolished at the Lausanne Conference of August 1932; so that Germany's need to find additional foreign exchange, or to make deliveries-in-kind, was reduced by a substantial percentage on this score.

In short, then, the Third Reich at the outset secured all the equipment 'lent' to the German Weimar Republic (in the form of the plant and services on which the former loans were spent); it had not to pay reparations; it had not to repay the full amounts borrowed; and its annual transfers of interest were greatly reduced. The losses were borne by the foreign creditors—both Governments who formerly received reparations and individuals or firms who, in order to realize at least some of what they had formerly lent to German firms or public bodies, took severe losses on the nominal capital value of their assets by offering them at big discounts to any buyer.

Thus it was that the Reich experts, led by Dr Schacht, were enabled to maintain for purposes of imports the Reichsmark at its pre-crisis parity of exchange. At the same time, for purposes of export from Germany or of transfer of foreign assets from Germany, the mark was, in effect, greatly depreciated. This acted as a subsidy to German exporters; so did the losses compulsorily suffered by foreign creditors of Germany. Germany's exporters were subsidized out of the various forms of 'blocked marks' sold by foreign creditors at a discount (that is, depreciated marks); and they were further subsidized, to enable them to secure export proceeds in foreign currencies, out of a levy on all industrial firms in Germany. The entire import-export trade of the Reich was placed under bureaucratic control, conducted on licences and permits. The Reich's needs of raw materials and foodstuffs were listed in order of importance; and the national economy of Germany speedily—in fact, by 1935—became authoritarian. The engagement and discharge of workers, the distribution of earnings in the shape of dividends and interest, the disposal of foreign assets held by German citizens, the production and sales programmes of individual firms, the book-keeping and bank accounts, savings banks and institutions, pension and sickness and unemployment insurance funds (both State and private)—all these elements in the conduct of German business came under the strict control of the Party-State and its organ, the Four-year Plan. On the workers' side the right to strike and to demand increased pay was virtually abolished, since the obverse of State pressure on the employer to retain workers and guarantee them security of tenure in their jobs was State pressure on workers to prevent them from interrupting production programmes, or jeopardizing the earnings which paid the State levies and taxes, by striking for shorter hours or more pay. The entire labour-force of the Reich was brought under the Labour Front, though, it is understood, at least one-third of the workers resented the system.

The industrialists and employers, big and small, who had thought in 1932 and 1933 that the Nazi Party would operate in their favour found that even if they made continuously increasing earnings and profits out of the Government's rearmament and public-works contracts, they were only permitted to declare dividends, and pay debenture interest, up to an average of about 6 per cent. and 5 per cent. respectively. All earnings over and above these figures had to be put into 'Government paper'— that is, bonds or bills, Government promises to pay, or IOU's—which thus provided the funds, in addition to greatly increased normal taxation and levies for export, for the large-scale rearmament and public-works contracts.

Moreover, on both workers and employers fell the burden of contributions to Party funds (ranked as voluntary), to the "Winter Help" for relief, despite absence of unemployment (that is, an indirect private subsidization of low-paid workers), and to the unemployment insurance fund (though there was progressively less and less officially recognized unemployment, and more and more contributors employed). In 1932 Chancellor Von Papen had instituted an ingenious financing system, whereby tax certificates issued by the authorities were made discountable by the Government against expectation of a rising revenue in the next four years. This system was taken over by the Nazi experts, who also extended the principle behind it. They proceeded, with Dr Schacht's advice and aid, to issue what were called Work-creation Bills or Rearmament Bills.

This method of financing by Government bills, or IOU's, needs examination; for on its understanding depends the answer to the oft-repeated query, " How does Germany *do* it all; and why doesn't she crack? "

The danger in putting out too many Government promises-to-pay is the same as in putting out too many banknotes. Both are promises-to-pay. If too many get out and pass into normal circulation—that is, are accepted as legal tender or as a medium of exchange in business or retail trade—then the supply of ' money ' (that is, of the medium for discharge of debt) will have increased beyond the current output of goods which people want. Up go the prices of the goods, for every one is competing for them before their supply can be in turn increased. If by the time that producers increase their supply the Government has in the meantime been steadily pumping out more and more ' money ' of one kind or another, the supply of goods will never catch up with the supply (and velocity of circulation) of money.

The vicious upward spiral of inflation will carry prices sky-high—as it did in Germany in 1922 and 1923. Now the Nazi experts, and the President of the Reichsbank, had cause to remember full well the effects of the disastrous German inflation of those years, the French invasion of the Ruhr which followed, and the borrowings from abroad which thereafter became necessary. They wanted to secure an 'advance' from the German workers and industrialists, without having recourse to the printing-press for money. Printing-press money would have immediately got into circulation. The way chosen was both simple and complicated. It was simple in theory, complicated in execution.

In theory it consisted in restricting both the purchasing power for consumable goods as *well* as the supply of those goods themselves, and in greatly expanding the production of non-consumable (' investment ' or ' capital ') goods.

In execution it meant that German industry had to receive orders and purchasing power from the Party-State to enable the production of armaments, public works, cement, steel, electricity, factories, etc.—all non-consumable goods—as well as the greatly increased man-power of the armed forces, Civil Service, and new bureaucracy, to be financed. Moreover, in execution this vast, State-initiated fillip to Germany's production of capital goods and public services could not be allowed to drive up wages or increase the volume of purchasing power relative to the volume of consumable goods; else inflationary signs would become evident in a rise of prices.

Accordingly the Party-State's control of labour conditions was used to lengthen hours of work, thus increasing output per man and per hourly wage. Its control of agriculture, industry, imports and exports, was used to restrict the supply of consumable goods and increase the supply of raw materials for industry. And its control of finance was used to draw in again (by levy, new taxes, voluntary contributions, enforced subscription to new issues of Government bonds or Work-creation Bills, etc.) the previously issued *industrial* purchasing power. This industrial or producers' purchasing power (not consumers') was put out in the form of State contracts and orders, which were paid for by issues of the bonds and bills.

Thus, as long as the system was successful in execution, the richer individuals and corporations could be made to bear increased direct taxes, to provide new funds to redeem old bills, and to put their bank deposits (over and above an agreed minimum) at the disposal of the State for subscription to new loans. The workers, on the other hand, had to contribute indirect taxes in the form of longer hours without higher wage-rates, compulsion to serve in labour-camps on purely nominal wages a day, shortages (often deliberately created and charged to the wickedness of rich and grasping foreigners) of certain foodstuffs like eggs, pig-meat, etc., and voluntary contributions to Party funds or Winter-help. Unemployment insurance contributions were taken from worker and employer alike, while employment rose until a shortage of labour appeared in 1938. Unemployment claims on the fund became negligible.

This provided more money. Moreover, a general, but equitably distributed, lowering of quality of all consumable goods took place. No one minded this, though all grumbled; for all had to suffer it together. As one German banker put it, " I cannot afford my car, or even one new, though shoddy, suit a year; but all my friends are in the same boat, so I don't feel ashamed." This, again, set free resources for use in the capital-construction programme.

The outcome was that the State-controlled investment programme raised net investment in the Reich from a minus quantity in 1932 and 1933 (that is, when Germany lived on its capital) to a figure in 1938 fully 50 per cent. above the 1929 level. Now, though the extraction of forced savings, such as we have described, from the German people and their conversion into armaments, new factories, highways, etc., can be called ' investment,' though much more is spent in turning out finished guns rather than butter, and though the increase in the production of capital goods always gives more employment and distributes more purchasing power than the same proportionate increase in production of consumable goods—yet there is a real danger in the rapidity with which the Nazi experts have engineered this extraordinary rise in national production, employment, income, and tax revenue. It can be stated in these terms.

First, Germany's national income (excluding Austria and the Sudeten regions) was only about equal in 1938 to its figure for 1928, a decade earlier.

Secondly, however, the burden of all forms of levy,

contribution, and taxation for the Party-State's purposes was practically double what it was in 1928–29.

Thirdly, owing to the vast State capital-construction programmes of 1934, 1935, and 1936, and to the continuous expansion of such programmes thereafter, a kind of bill is now beginning to be presented to the Party-State each year for renewals, maintenance, overhauls, repairs, and replacements not only of obsolete and obsolescent armaments, but also of railways, factories, plant, and vehicles whose owners and operators (whether private or public) have been compelled consistently to pare their allocations for such maintenance. Now, after five years of intense forced savings and investment in *new* capital, a kind of dilemma is emerging. Either the current programme for *new* capital construction must be curtailed by an amount necessary to maintain in proper efficiency the capital equipment built up in the last five years; or else, to maintain both the existing equipment and accelerate or expand the current programme of construction, new resources and new revenues must be found. To a certain extent, of course, every new programme creates its own new sources of revenue; as was explained above, the orders and contracts and payments awarded by the State can be ' milked ' by current increases of taxation, issues of new loans (to an amount exceeding the loans falling due for redemption), and levies. Also, no doubt—as long as the forces of dictatorship can be invoked without risk of serious discontent or disorder at home—the workers can be forced to yield more in output per hour; or their range of consumers' choice on what they spend their restricted wages can be once more narrowed, thus setting free more resources for investment or for exports that bring in necessary imports. But as fast, and as vast, as the Third Reich's capital equipment grows this third problem grows even faster and vaster. And the larger in the programme that armaments bulk, the less does the Reich's *productive* equipment increase. The more acute, therefore, becomes the dilemma, for it means that more and more of the new capital equipment is bespoke for the production of unproductive capital— i.e., guns rather than butter—and the more the normal, ' civil ' side of industry becomes burdened with the toll of providing the revenues to maintain the whole bulk at the level of full efficiency, and to ' carry ' the current construction.

Fourthly, the striking diplomatic victories attendant on the Third Reich's prowess in foreign affairs have brought the economic problems, described in preceding sections, of absorbing and assimilating within the Reich's authoritarian economic system the hitherto free economic systems of Austria and Czecho-Slovakia. New needs of capital and materials are created by these successes; and the integration of the Austrian and Sudeten industries with those of the Reich under the Four-year Plan will certainly be costly in the first few years of joint operation.

Lastly, the Reich of 80,000,000 souls has now to provide for a Reichswehr of 1,500,000 men, all abstracted for at least a year from the labour market. This is a peculiar danger in the German economy; for there began in 1938 an acute shortage of skilled labour in former

Germany—a shortage which has only been partly offset by the reservoirs of unemployed acquired in Austria and Czecho-Slovakia. Already in 1938 the women whom Field-Marshal Goering once relegated to the kitchen (and elsewhere) were being drawn back into factories and offices; and the allocation of some hundreds of thousands of young men and women to labour-service each year in itself dislocates the labour market. The increase in Reichswehr and labour-service conscripts each year after 1938, which is bound to become necessary, will add another element to the economic dilemma facing the Nazi authorities. That dilemma can be summarized in a query: to bring the Reich's economic system more and more completely under the State or to relax the sinews of warfare? The former will increase social tension in Germany; the latter will decrease the Reich's political and diplomatic potency abroad.

Some indication that these influences were already at work before even Austria was annexed can be gleaned from the following facts. In the winter of 1937–38 the recession in world trade had so imperilled Germany's ability to buy all her vital imports by means of her exports that the Reich authorities were selling in London, New York, Zürich, Amsterdam, etc.—that is, on every free foreign exchange centre—international and foreign bonds or shares formerly the property of German citizens, but impounded by the Nazi authorities. With the free currency proceeds in these centres the Reich then bought the strategic imports which it needed to complete its equipment programme.

Again, in March 1938 the issue and renewal of the

Work-creation Bills ceased. These bills had always been discountable at the Reichsbank—that is, a firm or bank taking up a bill and paying the Reich authorities for it could always raise money on it by taking it, before due date, to the Reichsbank. The bills, however, though falling due, were always renewed; so that in effect they constituted a revolving, but steadily expanding, State credit. After March 1938 the issue of new Work-creation Bills was stopped, while the total amount kept on revolving; but a new series of bills was put out under the direct control of the Finance Ministry. These were six-months bills; they were not discountable at all; they could only be sold outright to the market by the firms and persons who had originally taken them up. Concurrently, and in increasing amounts during the rest of 1938, the Reich authorities began to issue new public long-term loans at attractive terms (for example, with relatively near dates for redemption), most of which were taken up by insurance corporations, Reich institutions, banks, and big industrial concerns, which put their liquid reserves or available resources into them. The conjunction of these events—cessation of the issue of new Work-creation Bills, issue of new non-discountable bills under the Finance Ministry, and resumption of direct Government borrowing from the public—indicated that the Work-creation Bill system had tapped off all the available resources of big industrial concerns, that the floating debt thus created in five years had become top-heavy, that the proceeds of new loans would partly be used to consolidate the top-heavy floating debt, and that (as was evidenced in the acute shortage of skilled labour) there was some risk of inflation. Meanwhile the supply and prices of consumers' goods had scarcely risen since 1933, so the workers scented no danger. On top of these financial problems came the annexation of the Austrian and Czecho-Slovak territories, with its concomitant economic requirements.

The Third Reich's main preoccupation from the outset—indeed, one of the chief causes of the Nazi Party's advent to power—was the weakness of Germany's foreign trading position. The vast German industrial machine, brought up to date by large-scale German borrowing between 1924 and 1929, had to be fed. It was all to the good that the Party-State ' blocked ' transfers of principal and interest to Germany's foreign creditors, forced down the price of German bonds abroad and then bought them back at low prices (that is, reduced Germany's foreign indebtedness), paid no more reparations, and practically kept the " Standstill " funds revolving as a credit for purchases from abroad. But in maintaining the nominal parity of the Reichsmark out of fear of the social effects of another inflation—and devaluation would have led the German people to ascribe it, and the risk of inflation, to the recently victorious Nazis—the astute Dr Schacht was faced with the most difficult of all his problems.

How was he to increase German exports to pay for the increased German imports for the armament programme, without devaluing the Reichsmark? The world's leading currencies were already greatly devalued. If he did not devalue, some method of expanding German exports, to pay for the increasing imports, was imperatively called for; moreover, a method was required which should preferably make the foreigner pay the cost. We have mentioned the way in which he subsidized exports out of the foreign creditors' losses in marks. We have also mentioned the levy on all German industry. But there was yet another way of mulcting the 'foreigner.' This was to secure most of Germany's vital imports from the smaller countries which individually could not exert equal bargaining power in trade relations with Germany. Accordingly, after 1933 first Dr Schacht's own Ministry of Economics, and then the office of the Four-year Plan under Field-Marshal Goering, began and conducted an intensive trade drive in Central and South-eastern Europe, Latin America, the Low Countries, Switzerland, Scandinavia, and the Baltic states. The maintenance of the German mark nominally at its former parity, and the agreements with her creditors, had forced Germany to place much of her foreign trade under ' clearing agreements ' with each particular foreign country. This meant that the Reich was only able to import up to the amount of the goods which she exported to each country. Exceptions were Britain, France, the U.S.A., and a few other countries to which she exported more than she took from them. In these exceptional countries she always obtained a surplus of free foreign exchange, which she could use to settle her bills with countries like Canada, from whom she imported more than she exported to them. Thus, with only about £25,000,000 of free foreign exchange per annum—that is, the proceeds of German exports—to play with in a few centres, the Reich authorities began to place large orders—but not to pay—for the foodstuffs, fodder, timber, oil, metals, ores, coffee, and tobacco of smaller countries like Holland, Denmark, Sweden, Finland, Poland, Hungary, Rumania, Jugoslavia, Greece, Bulgaria, Turkey, Lithuania, Latvia, and Estonia. The net was spread as far as Brazil and Chile.

Alone Austria and Czecho-Slovakia, because their finances and currencies were sound, declined to participate in the new German system of bilateral trade, with its accompaniments of clearing, barter, and compensation agreements. Their exports to, and imports from, Germany ranged from 13 to 17 per cent. of their total foreign trade; they were less dependent on Germany than any other small state.

The smaller countries at first jumped at the German orders, especially as the orders were in bulk and for long contractual terms. These countries, especially those of Danubia, had surpluses to sell; there was a slump in world trade; the normal import markets of western countries were being steadily closed to their products in favour of domestic producers or producers in their empires; and their domestic, political, and economic stability, as well as their currencies, depended on an export surplus—to say nothing of the annual services of their foreign debts, for they were almost all debtor nations. To orders for existing and future surpluses of their products the Nazi economic authorities added requests that special products should be grown—for example, soya-beans in Hungary, Jugoslavia, and Rumania. The Governmental authorities in the Danubian countries complied, for Germany up to 1929 was their chief customer. Up to 1938 she had contrived to increase her share of the exports from each country; and after 1938 the 'pull' of the former Austrian and Czecho-Slovak markets was added to Germany's existing 'pull' on the smaller countries round Germany. Though Germany, however, had greatly increased her *shares* of each smaller country's exports, the total *volume* of her imports from her neighbours in 1937 was not as great as it had been in 1929, owing to the slump in world trade, the redirection of Germany's own trade, and the lessened export capacity of many of the smaller countries.

Like the British Dominions and colonies with Britain, the Danubian and Balkan States did much more trade with Germany than among themselves. This was partly because they exported mainly the same commodities. The slump after 1930 led to excesses of economic nationalism, which reduced their trade among themselves, but intensified competition among them for the big import markets of the world; and of these Germany was nearest.

The expanded Third Reich's normal needs of cereals after 1938 (in good years her needs of wheat and oats are least important, though in bad years they are considerable) can be covered by the export surpluses of Poland, Hungary, Jugoslavia, Bulgaria, Rumania, and Turkey, though Greece needs to import all kinds of cereals. If the Third Reich after 1938 took *all* the export surpluses of cattle, pigs, pig-meat, and ordinary meat from all the countries mentioned above it still would need more, for the Austrian and Czecho-Slovak deficiencies are added to former Germany's needs. If the Third Reich after

1938 took *all* the tobacco exports of Greece, Turkey, Bulgaria, Jugoslavia, and Hungary it would still need a little more. The Reich's need of dairy products can be covered by the export surpluses of Holland, Denmark, Poland, Hungary, and Jugoslavia, though the annexation of the Austrian and Sudeten regions increases its need of eggs, of which there has long been a deficiency in former Germany. The new Third Reich and every other country in the list, except Poland and Rumania, together need to import about 5,500,000 metric tons of petroleum and oils in a year, whereas Poland's small surplus (about 125,000 tons) and Rumania's large one (7,000,000 tons) could cover this joint need of Central Europe and the Balkans entire.

On the other hand, Rumanian and German authorities signed an agreement in Bucharest in December 1938 whereby Germany is to receive an increased share in Rumania's oil exports, which will, even so, amount only of 25 per cent. of all Rumania's oil exports. As the new Reich's import requirements in a year are still about 4,000,000 tons it will have to find at least another 2,000,000 tons elsewhere—making generous allowance for the Reich's increased ability to produce oil from the new Sudeten coal deposits. Turkey alone produces a surplus of cotton, but not one-seventh of the new Reich's requirements. No single country exports jute or wool; indeed, all import them. In flax and hemp Germany can cover her requirements in the Baltic states, Poland, Hungary, and Jugoslavia, but only if she takes virtually the entire surpluses of these countries, for the newly acquired Austrian and Sudeten industries have doubled her former needs. It will be remarked that in many cases the Reich will need to take all of the surpluses of these countries. This would upset their trade and that of existing clients. Moreover, all these countries must preserve a large portion of their exports for sale in ' free-currency ' countries (for example, Britain, U.S.A., France, Holland, Switzerland). Otherwise they cannot import the raw materials from overseas. And if Germany takes *all* their exports then Germany will have to procure and send them raw materials—not German manufactures, which would force Germany to ' carry the baby ' for them.

In the strategically more important commodities the new Reich has a surplus only in coal, graphite, and magnesite. But Poland, after acquiring the Teschen area, now has a surplus of coal almost one-half that of the Reich's. Poland's, Hungary's, and Rumania's requirements of iron ore completely swamp the small surpluses of Greece, Jugoslavia, and Bulgaria; and the new Reich is left to cover its enormous needs—three times her home production, despite the new State works based on low-grade domestic ores—in Sweden, Lorraine, and Nationalist Spain. Greek nickel can supply about 30 per cent. of the Reich's needs; but in the cases of copper, lead, zinc, pyrites, manganese, phosphates, and tin the Reich will still be overwhelmingly dependent on other countries than those of Central and South-eastern Europe and Turkey. In the cases of chrome ore and antimony the total export surpluses of Turkey and Greece can supply all its needs. And if the Reich can command the entire export surpluses of bauxite in

Hungary, Jugoslavia, Italy, and Greece, it will still need to cover one-fifth of its requirements (for aluminium) elsewhere.

Accordingly the new Reich can only become partially self-sufficient, even on the combined export surpluses of all Eastern, Central and South-eastern Europe; and there is no reason to suppose that countries like Rumania, Greece, Turkey, Bulgaria, Jugoslavia—to ignore Poland, Hungary, and the rump Czecho-Slovakia —will, apart from sheer military conquest, rapidly turn over their *entire* exports to the Reich.

In 1929 Germany took the following percentage shares of each of these countries' exports: Poland, 31 per cent.; Hungary, 12 per cent.; Rumania, 28 per cent.; Jugoslavia, 8 per cent.; Bulgaria, 30 per cent.; Greece, 23 per cent.; and Turkey, 13 per cent. In 1937 these shares had become, respectively, 14 per cent., 26 per cent., 21 per cent., 21 per cent., 42 per cent., 27 per cent., and 36 per cent. The annexation of Austria and the Sudetenland are estimated to have changed the share of Poland's exports going to the new Third Reich into 21 per cent., of Hungary's to 46 per cent., of Rumania's to 31 per cent., of Jugoslavia's to 38 per cent., of Bulgaria's to 53 per cent., of Greece's to 33 per cent., and of Turkey's to 42 per cent. It will be noted that the Reich's share of their export trade has, on the whole, doubled since 1929, though the volume is now roughly the same, allowance being made for the recent annexations. The explanation of all this is that by contracting to take more of each smaller country's exports the Reich was able rapidly to assume preponderant importance in each

country's economy. It ran up a heavy bill for the purchases, and then pushed German wares, at relatively
higher prices than those of goods which might have been
purchased on free-currency markets (if the smaller
country's exports could have been sold there). Faced
with mounting commercial credits in Germany, the
result of the increased earlier exports to that country,
the smaller countries could only unfreeze such 'blocked
balances' in three ways: (a) by acquiring property in
Germany; (b) by buying from an arbitrarily determined
list of German goods at arbitrarily fixed prices; and (c)
by accepting from the German financial authorities at or
near their full nominal value the bonds which each
smaller country had issued to foreign creditors in earlier
years, and which the German authorities had contrived
to buy up on foreign centres.

No country elected to follow device (a). Most of them
were compelled to import large quantities of a limited
range of German 'civil' goods, extending from photo-
graphic apparatus, chemicals, harmonicas, typewriters, to
bust-bodices and aspirin—which led an American wit to
remark that there was a chronic over-supply of these
goods in each Balkan country, but an under-supply of
typists and headaches. One or two countries elected to
repatriate, out of their 'blocked balances' in Reichsmarks, that part of their external debt represented by
their foreign bonds which the German authorities had
bought up cheaply. Finally, not on the 'civil' side of
business, these countries could buy obsolescent or redundant armaments from Germany.

This process itself, however, was beginning to exhaust

its uses by 1938. For one thing, the smaller suppliers of Germany realized that the security and stability of large, long-term contracts with the Reich were being dearly bought—not only in terms of the manufactures received in exchange. If, as actually occurred, a Balkan capital city awarded contracts for housing, bridge-building, gas and electricity and sanitation installations, to German firms, a body of German experts would promptly descend on the locality and chart the minutiæ of the city's strategic points. If Hungary, Jugoslavia, and Rumania agreed to lay down soya-bean plantations then the extensive and costly equipment for crushing, extraction, and preparation could only be obtained from Germany, where the giant chemical trust, the I.G. Farbenindustrie, held all the patents and specifications. If the domestic railways, iron- and steel-works, bus and tram services, and armed forces placed orders for equipment in the Reich, in order to unfreeze blocked balances, which continuously mounted as German orders for these smaller countries' raw materials or foodstuffs increased, then those strategic domestic concerns became dependent on German industry for renewals and maintenance. If, on the other hand, as Hungary and Jugoslavia attempted to do in 1937 and 1938, these countries demanded that exports to Germany should be equal to imports from Germany in any one year, the German authorities could exercise two distinct threats: (a) that the blocked balances would never be liquidated at all—that is, the small country to whose credit they stood would have been expropriated of its former exports which had given rise to the balances; and (b) that German orders, accounting for so great a proportion of her export trade, would instantly be transferred to another country. As all these small countries were primary producers, with peasant populations living at a bare subsistence level and with vulnerable State finances, the fear of grave social and political disorders thereby conjured up by the German authorities—the Nazi Party, in addition, had its agents in each country—was sufficient to bring them to heel. Thus, by clearings, barter agreements, and compensation trade, the Third Reich had by the end of 1938 imposed a kind of stranglehold on the economic systems of virtually every country lying between Germany, Russia, and the Ægean Sea.

Nevertheless, the structure of the Reich's vast European commercial dominion was not free from cracks and fissures. The array of small client states needed raw materials themselves—rubber, tin, cotton, wool, coffee, iron ore, colonial produce, hides, jute, and (except Rumania) oil. They needed, in addition, manufactures and semi-manufactures like agricultural machinery, fertilizers, yarns, vehicles, industrial plant; some of them needed ships; and all of them needed development capital, either in the form of funds to spend in many separate countries supplying equipment or else in the shape of the industrial equipment itself. All Eastern, Central, and South-eastern Europe requires either more and better highways or else more and modernized railways. The incidence of a combined demand of this magnitude upon the already internally strained economy of the Third Reich is too burdensome to be borne, except over many years. It can only be borne quickly if the Reich's programme for continuous development of its own sinews of warfare is severely curtailed—which seems improbable. Accordingly Germany after 1938, facing many new and some old internal economic problems, cannot greatly increase her hold on the output of the Danubian and associated countries unless —and it is a big ' unless '—she incorporates their entire economic systems within that of the new Third Reich. She cannot meet all their raw-material requirements, all their capital requirements, all their needs of equipment—and simultaneously turn the ever-expanding Reich into a more and more potent war-machine at home.

For example, in 1937 of the total trade of Hungary, Rumania, Jugoslavia, Bulgaria, and Greece together, while about 40 per cent. was with Germany and Austria, about 20 per cent. was with Britain, France, and the U.S.A.

If we add all Czecho-Slovakia's foreign trade to that of Germany and Austria the three countries would still account for less than 50 per cent. of the five South-east European states. Finally, if we look upon the new Reich, the new Czecho-Slovakia, and Italy as one trading unit—which they certainly are not yet—the rest of the world accounts for between 40 and 50 per cent. of the total foreign trade of Poland, Hungary, Jugoslavia, Bulgaria, Rumania, Greece, and Turkey. These latter countries export to the rest of the world, apart from the German-Italian system, raw materials and foodstuffs; and if their total exports were taken by the German-Italian system they would still have to import *other* raw materials for their own needs, which the German-Italian system would have to find.

Thus we can at once discern one danger to the rest of the world in further German (or German-Italian) economic expansion to the east and south-east.

It is that the German authorities might attempt to corner all the supplies from these European countries, send them the equipment they need in exchange, and—this is the crux—act as a vast *entrepôt* centre for all Europe beyond the Rhine and Alps. Over and above East and South-east Europe's needs of equipment, which the Reich might conceivably supply (granted the maintenance of peace), the Reich might become the *marketing agency* for all these countries' surpluses, selling them to the outside world, and buying from the outside world whatever raw materials (for example, rubber, wool, oil, nickel, cotton, coffee, tin, iron ore) they themselves require. If this were set in operation the Reich could only be sure of obtaining the necessary raw materials *from* the outside world if it were equally sure of disposing *to* the outside world of all East and South-east Europe's products not required in Germany or Italy. The Reich can only be sure of that by doing one thing —that is, ensuring its sales abroad. This means that, at all costs, the Reich's own manufactures, and the surpluses obtained from its client states, must be sold. And this means, in turn, that the Reich would always, in the last analysis, be underselling its keenest competitor. The implications for the outside world need no emphasis.

That something like this was already feared at the

end of 1938 was evident in the British Government's announcement in December of the enlargement of the Export Credit Fund's facilities from £50,000,000 to £75,000,000, and of the extension by an additional £10,000,000 of guarantees to aid British exporters in markets where subsidized German exports were forging ahead for political purposes. If certain British exports were deemed politically important they would rank for financial guarantee under this ten-million-pound extension of facilities.

This British reaction to Germany's economic ' forward policy' in South-eastern Europe was sudden and unexpected. It followed hard on the heels of pronouncements by the Reich Minister for Economics, Dr Walter Funk, during his tour of the Balkans in September and October 1938. Dr Funk then claimed that the Reich was " free of " the world economic system, pointed out that Germany did not bother about foreign exchange, money, and credit, and made the significant statement that " economic policy cannot be separated from general political policy." His visit to Turkey resulted in a 'credit' from Germany to that country of R.M. 150,000,000 (say £8,000,000) for the purchase of German industrial and military equipment, to be repaid over ten years; and this was within five months of the British Government's credit of £16,000,000 to the Turkish Government for naval and industrial equipment. Such German credits differ considerably from what is usually understood by the term. When the Reich increased its imports from all the smaller countries by more than it exported to them, and so added to their blocked balances in Germany, the financial authorities in each small state could not pay their own producers with blocked marks. Their central banks, therefore, had to advance funds, in the local currency, until imports from Germany rose high enough to give Germany credits in the local currency. Then, in theory, the blocked balances in Germany would have been offset by Germany's credit in each small country. But—and here was the rub—the German authorities empowered German contracting firms to 'grant' long-term credits to these smaller countries for the large-scale works (bridges, buildings, equipment) which had only been allotted to German firms in order to unfreeze the blocked balances in Germany. Consequently the blocked balances which had arisen from exports to Germany, already delivered, were only unfrozen very slowly, over the period of years covered by the German credit so kindly ' granted.'

The result was that the smaller countries' banking and financial institutions had to stand in the gap, for the local farmers, peasants, miners, and workers had to be paid. They had delivered their products to Germany, and could not wait for payment until the German ' credit ' had been finally repaid by the local firm, or municipality, or even Government which had awarded a German firm the contract. Such, in many a case, was the kind of ' credit ' granted by the Reich. It was, in fact, a credit to one institution in the smaller country, at the expense of the central bank, or other institution, of the same state.

Clearly there was no end to this kind of robbing of

Peter to pay Paul. If only one Paul claimed payment of blocked balances at a time, and the supply of potential Peters was extensive, the German system of trading on other people's credit could go on indefinitely. It would only stop if all Peters became Pauls simultaneously. This they never did, owing to the serious threat to each of their social, political, and economic structures which German refusal to take their exports would have constituted.

But the British financial initiative raised a very real threat to Germany. If in addition to bulk purchases of foodstuffs, such as those undertaken by the British authorities in the autumn of 1938 (when, among other similar transactions, half of Rumania's wheat surplus was bought by Britain), the British authorities began to subsidize their own exporters to compete with German methods, a different picture would be presented. For British financial resources were adequate and liquid. Germany's were either tied up, bespoke for vital imports, or limited by the extent of the blocked balances standing to each small client state's credit account in Germany. Once the smaller countries of East and Southeast Europe saw the *possibility* of securing sterling for their exports—that is, importing British goods and then selling their own goods to Britain in payment—they would gradually go over to the 'sterling area' of trade. Sterling could be used to buy anything anywhere; blocked marks were restricted to a given list of German exports, costly in comparison with other goods and deteriorating in quality.

At the end of 1938 there was, therefore, both in

Britain and Germany, a realization that a 'war of subsidies' was on the verge of breaking out. The visit of Dr Schacht to Mr Montagu Norman, Governor of the Bank of England, in the middle of December, was freely rumoured to be in connexion with this possibility, as well as to secure financial concessions to enable Jews to leave the Reich.

It would seem obvious that the financial and trading systems of the Third Reich had by the close of 1938 encountered severe obstacles. These problems were only partly due to the expansion of the Reich over Austria and Czecho-Slovakia. They were in no small measure due to the awareness alike of German intentions and German methods in every client state. They were intensified by the counter-measures threatened by Germany's competitors, the domestic requirements of rearmament in Germany, and the sudden awareness in Germany of the magnitude of the financial and trading problems after 1938. On the one hand, the brilliant successes of the Reich in diplomacy had increased its potential economic advantages. On the other, the translation of these potentialities into realities demanded peace, order, and the "inevitability of gradualness." If these conditions were not met—suppose, for example, that the Reich charged headlong into a major war—then it would not be sure of the economic or political allegiance of all the countries which it hoped to utilize as client states. It would not, as yet, be able to command *all* their economic resources without extending over them such an array of military control as would render its conduct of the war perilous, its risk of defeat considerable.

Moreover, the British and French economic systems were in better shape to face a protracted war than the German and Italian. If the Axis Powers were militarily more prepared for war it was to be a 'lightning war' with a 'lightning' victory. Otherwise, the lesser military machines of Britain and France would progressively become strengthened from their greater economic resources, while the Italo-German economic resources became progressively more strained. France and Britain in 1938 were together making one-third less steel than were Italy and the new Reich; but the two Western Powers' domestic and overseas supplies of iron ore, copper, nickel, tin, bauxite, rubber, chrome ore, manganese, wolfram, tungsten, and petroleum were far larger than the new Reich and Italy together could command in all Europe east of the Rhine and Alps. Behind Britain and France, as long as they shared command of the Atlantic and (at the least) the Western Mediterranean, were the vast reservoirs of raw materials and foodstuffs in their overseas dominions and all America. In the British Commonwealth of Nations alone were thirty-two out of the thirty-seven chief industrial raw materials. The Commonwealth had a monopoly of the supply of jute and nickel, and a dominant position in the supply of lead, tin, rubber, wool, asbestos, and palm oil. Its deficiencies were only in sulphur, soya-beans, olive oil, molybdenum (a steel-hardening substance), and hemp; and the French Empire covered many of these deficiencies.

Against this formidable economic array the new Reich and Italy together—if together they would stand—could muster only 50 per cent. more man-power; surpluses of coal, sulphur, mercury, magnesite, graphite, and sugar; and the overwhelming economic deficiencies already described.

Moreover, to these deficiencies—which would exist even if both the Axis Powers held undisputed sway over all Europe beyond the Rhine and Alps, including the entire Eastern Mediterranean—must be added the domestic, financial, and economic problems of Italy and the new Reich: the now-emergent problem of maintaining existing armaments while expanding current output; the problem of developing their trade with, and the resources of, client states; the problem of meeting intensified competition in foreign markets; the problem of raising their own national incomes while increasing the toll of ever-expanding armaments upon those incomes; the problem of finding funds to maintain and expand 'civil' industrial equipment, to feed the armaments industries; the problem of taxable capacity among their home populations. If their military and economic resources have been organized to win 'lightning' victories they cannot engage in—though in their diplomatic campaigns they may risk starting—a war of economic attrition. If their joint and several diplomatic campaigns risk war, but gain victories because others keep the peace, so much the better for them. If they risk war, but do not gain victories, then they must accept either defeat in diplomacy or defeat in war. Such, at least, is the conclusion to which our analysis of their economic position at the end of 1938 leads us.

Finally, since the Third Reich is now dominant over

Italy economically, strategically, and politically, Germany alone becomes the decisive factor east of the Rhine and Alps. Much time, much labour, much capital, will be required to weld all the economic resources of the New Danubia into an effective and reliable storehouse or power-house for the Third Reich. The amount of time it will need depends on the intensity with which the Reich puts in the labour and equipment. But Germany's labour, her equipment, are both limited and already earmarked for other, non-productive uses. And until she has subjugated, and reduced beneath her economic and political and military sway, most of the small nations between her frontiers, Russia, and the Ægean Sea, she cannot seriously threaten the Western Powers with war. Not seriously, because she may still feel militarily strong enough to *threaten* war as an adjunct of diplomacy, without intending to invoke it if the demands of her diplomacy are refused. (The return of her colonies, for instance, would give her strategic advantages without increasing her economic resources or staying-power; indeed, they would necessitate an expansion in her naval programme and her programme for the construction of strategic air and naval bases.) It is to the Third Reich's obvious interest to consolidate its economic gains, to organize them for the ends which diplomacy sets before it, and to render the Reich (and its Axis partner) immune, as far and as quickly as possible, from defeat by a war of attrition with the two Western Powers. If this can be accomplished—as it may well be in two or three or a few more years—then the ever-expanding Third Reich may count either on speedy victory in a lightning war against the West, or an infinitely more costly stalemate—but still a stalemate—in a war of attrition. And that would mean that Germany, and the German dominion of the New Danubia, would in either case dictate the destinies of Europe entire.

For such a consummation, however, the Reich must be absolutely and utterly sure of political and military control over all the countries around her eastern and south-eastern borders, right down to Asia Minor. Without such control this New Danubia cannot be made to function as Germany's economic granary and powerhouse. After five years of scarcely precedented economic effort the Reich has been able to secure valuable strategic and political acquisitions. From now on economics wait upon political and military control by the Reich of all Eastern, Central, and South-eastern Europe. Without that the Reich's present economic power will not suffice.

Thus, our earlier analysis of the strategic factors in Central Europe after 1938 led us to examine the economic factors; and, paradoxically, our analysis of the economic changes and influences has led us back to the military and political factors. This is not as surprising nor as elusive a quest as it may appear; for there is scarcely a single economic problem of statecraft to-day which requires no political action and has no political effects. Nor is there any political action which does not acquire economic significance, does not have some economic outcome. Our conclusions will emerge from a study of both these forces, the economic and the political, in the new Europe beyond Germany. How these two influences shape Danubian destiny will determine the destiny of the entire Continent. Behind us are facts. How are they shaping what lies before us?

THE RAILWAYS OF CENTRAL AND SOUTH-EASTERN EUROPE, JANUARY 1939

PART III

POLITICS AND POWERS

(i) *The Danubian Question*

AFTER examining the extent and effects of the abrupt
changes in Central, Eastern, and South-east Europe in
1938 we have to assess their political worth.

In the new geographical and political frontiers, in the
redistribution of population and man-power, in the
altered strategic lay-out of all Europe beyond the Rhine
and Alps, and in the sudden and far-reaching economic
change which came over the bulk of Europe in 1938 we
have been faced with a formidable array of new facts, by
which our thinking must be readjusted. But, having
tried to effect that readjustment, we must not fall into
the error of resting content with accomplished facts, as
if, being past, they were bound to remain steadfast and
unmovable. The great changes of 1938 were achieved
by diplomacy, prepared by politics, executed by military
threats; so by threats, politics, and diplomacy can they
be modified or even undone.

If European civilization is no longer a unity that is
because there has been no unified system of international
good behaviour between Europe's sovereign states since
1932. Consequently the violent upset in 1938 of the
entire European balance of power, though very unfavourable to Britain and France in the diplomatic, military,
and strategic spheres, may not in itself be a sound and
durable achievement.

On the one hand, of course, the domination of Europe beyond the Rhine and Alps by the Third Reich may be beneficial—if that Reich suffers a change of heart, and decides, or is compelled by changes yet to occur, to re-enter the unitary European system of plain dealing, straightforward trade and diplomacy, and of sincere collaboration to maintain peace and raise the material welfare of all Europe's peoples. On the other hand, if Germany, with or without Italy, proceeds to capitalize the great gains of 1938 in an exclusive and drastically organized system of warlike preparations and economic exploitation, then not only European peace will be uneasy, ill-founded, and unreliable. European diplomacy, the demeanour of one nation before another, the production of trade of the largest industrial area in the world, the desires and passions of 450,000,000 Europeans, and their domestic political stresses and strains—all these will become more, instead of less, undependable; more, instead of less, fiercely and unyieldingly intense.

If we take all the new facts we have been forced to face, look back into the history of Europe, and try to estimate what new influences have been evoked or liberated in the New Danubia, we shall, perhaps, be surprised how little has been altered in a thousand years. The population of all Europe has grown enormously, and standards of living have risen. But the barbarians who broke down the Western Roman Empire have divided among themselves. Part, as in England, became a mongrel stock, constantly cross-fertilized. Part are more Latinized Frankish or Gothic or Lombardic nations, like Italy and France and Spain. Part have remained intensely and tribally Teutonic, like the Germans throughout Europe. (Italian Fascismo's claims to be 'Roman' are not as justified as France's might be, for Italy, we must remember, is more Teutonic in the northern half of its population than ever France was.) The Slav barbarians, after obtaining virtually the dominion of all Eastern Europe from the Arctic Circle down to the Ægean Sea (in which process they pushed well into Germany, accounting for as much as one-third of the population of Prussia), were themselves caught between two fires—the Germans in the west and the Turks or Tartars in the south-east and east. The history of the Slavs, who now account for almost one-third of Europe's population, has been nothing but the erection and speedy collapse of vast Slav empires, nothing but subjugation to either a German (Prussian or Austrian) or a Turkish yoke, punctuated by violent rebellions. Thus, after the Liberal nationalism of the nineteenth century had undone the enlightened despotism of the seventeenth and eighteenth, which had subjugated the Slavs, the war of 1914–18 enabled them to set up the nations and frontiers of their dreams. Yet again has the pendulum of history swung back; and within twenty years of 1918 the twentieth-century age of unenlightened despotism, of the divine right of race and State and leaders, has begun to threaten all the Slavs of Europe with subjugation once again. This time subjugation might equally be German or Caucasian, German or Russian—perhaps one could even say German or Asiatic, for the Slav element in Russia was being slowly superseded.

The destiny which after 1938 began to unfold before all Europe between Germany-Italy and Russia as the familiar map was rolled up was therefore not in itself unfamiliar. For instance, it is interesting to note that both in the Third Reich and in its supposedly most hated enemy, the Soviet Union, the clearest and most shocking, most surprising characteristics of the governing oligarchy are the personal despotism, ostentatious adulation, reliance upon Pretorian Guards, the luxury of the oligarchs under the Leader, the summary personal justice—all of which are the very opposite of the ascetic Protestant Prussians' characteristics, the virtues that built up Prussia, or those of the equally ascetic, frugal, thoroughly collective-minded Slavs. There are many similar characteristics displayed by the oligarchs of the Nazi Party and the Soviet Union. They are Asiatic characteristics.

The Slavs of Europe, as was pointed out earlier, have no love for either form of personal or oligarchic despotism. Yet once again they are caught between two fires; and their only hope of safety lies in a closing of all the Slav ranks in Eastern and South-eastern Europe: Baltic states with Poland and Russia, Czecho-Slovakia with the Slavs of Rumania, and so round to Bulgaria and Jugoslavia. This they cannot yet accomplish, for, apart from the ideological split in Europe which puts Russia out of court for the time being, Poland and Czecho-Slovakia have been and still are at loggerheads over Teschen; the autonomy of the (Slav) Ukrainians is a thorny question for Poland, Czecho-Slovakia, Rumania, and Russia; Jugoslavia is caught between

Germany and Italy on one front, and the German and Italian friends, the Hungarians, on the other; Bulgaria has claims against Rumania. The revisionistic aspirations of non-Slav Hungary, in the very centre of the Danubian Basin, are supported by Germany and Italy; those of Bulgaria against Rumania might be realized with the help of German pressure on Rumania *via* Czecho-Slovak Ruthenia and Hungary. Thus Germany and Italy can use pressure on non-Slav and Slav, can profit by one Slav nation's grievance against another, can utilize the mutilated and defenceless new Czecho-Slovakia as a springboard from which to take new plunges into the Slav sea.

For these reasons it is important that we should bear in mind all the geographical, racial, strategic, and economic changes in 1938 before we set out to describe, analyse, and assess the changed political influences on the new Central European states. The main question is: How far will Eastern, Central, and South-eastern Europe be an extension of German, or German-Italian, political power? To answer it we must obviously take as much account of internal politics in each country concerned as of the political relations between them. We shall find that all the changes we have already studied will exert political influence in each country, on the relations between them, and on the entire European balance of power. It is in this context that Danubian destiny becomes conterminous with Europe's destiny. Let us, therefore, pass in rapid review the position in which the Central and South-east European countries find themselves after Munich.

(ii) *The New Czecho-Slovakia*

The extent of the political revolution which Munich accomplished in Czecho-Slovakia is best gauged by the resignation of President Beneš. This resignation was a recognition that the dependence of Czecho-Slovakia upon the two western democratic Great Powers, and on the League of Nations which they headed, was changed into dependence on Germany. Though the new President, Dr Hacha, was a democratic and eminent jurist, the new Government began its work by 'purging' State offices of adherents to the policy of the two great Presidents, Masaryk and Beneš. An anti-Semitic movement and programme was launched in deference to German susceptibilities; the Communist Party was dissolved; Communist and Socialist newspapers were confiscated and banned; a drastic Press censorship prevented publication of anything uncongenial to Germany; and a *régime* of " authoritarian democracy," as it was called, was inaugurated.

The new Czecho-Slovak Government itself was testimony to the degree of the new state's dependence on Germany. As a result of dismemberment of the former state in favour of Germany, Poland, and Hungary, Slovakia and Ruthenia were granted autonomy within a new federal state. But at the centre the Slovaks and Ruthenians naturally had to be represented. This gave rise to a serious fissure in the structure of internal politics, for the Nazi Party in Germany had long supported the autonomists of Slovakia, who until his death in the early summer of 1938 were led by Father Hlinka.

When the Reich incorporated the Sudeten and other regions, and thus gave Slovakia the power to obtain autonomy, control of Slovakia was handed over to the Hlinka Guards, a para-military formation headed by a prominent Slovak autonomist, M. Sidor. The Guard was organized on Nazi lines—even their uniforms were composed of Nazi, Fascist, and pre-War Hungarian elements; and no effective opposition to the Guard in Slovakia was possible. Accordingly the Nazi Party was able, thenceforth, to exercise *in Prague*, as well as in the Slovak capital, Bratislava, a powerful leverage on internal Czecho-Slovak politics. If the Czechs in Prague showed evidence of independent conduct the Slovak Guard and its leader, M. Sidor, could be relied upon to bring pressure—amounting to a threat of complete secession from the new federal state and a junction with Hungary—on the Cabinet. At the same time, in Bratislava, the development of autonomous Slovakia was inspired and often planned by Reich Nazis. The position of more moderate Slovaks, like the successor to Father Hlinka, M. Tiso, was compromised by the presence and activities of the Hlinka Guardsmen.

On the other hand, the Reich had retained Ruthenia —a very small and uneconomic rump Ruthenia—for the new Czecho-Slovakia; and here, too, in the new autonomous province (at the little village of Chust, which was all that was left to the new Ruthenia as a capital) the Nazis set up political and trade bureaux and a military mission. The latter was necessitated by the Polish-Hungarian plan, devised long before Munich in case of a dismemberment of the former Czecho-Slovakia, to incorporate all Ruthenia in Hungary, so as to give Poland and Hungary a common frontier around Germany and the new state of Czecho-Slovakia. But though at Vienna in November 1938 the Italian and German arbitrators (the two Foreign Ministers, Herr von Ribbentrop and Count Ciano) between Hungary and the new Czecho-Slovakia awarded Hungary only the richer, southern portions of Slovakia and Ruthenia, and retained a rump Ruthenia dividing Poland from Hungary, it was necessary for the Reich to mobilize almost three army corps on the Polish-Silesian-Czech frontier, and to take strong diplomatic action in Budapest, to prevent a surprise attack on Ruthenia by Polish and Hungarian ' irregulars ' or ' volunteers.' The Polish-Hungarian plan was foiled and put into cold storage. But the outcome was that the strategic Ruthenian corridor into Rumania and the Polish-Russian Ukraine, with its new Ruthenian-Rumanian-Russian railway described earlier, remained under the uneasy joint control of Hungary and Czecho-Slovakia. Consequently it became as urgent for Nazi influence to prevail in Budapest as in Prague if ever that corridor were to be utilized for military purposes.

The new Government in Prague was also completely different from former Czecho-Slovak Governments. It was overwhelmingly composed of those Right-wing Czech Agrarians who had long opposed the Masaryk-Beneš policy of collaboration and collective security between democracies. These Agrarians had always been friendly disposed to Nazi Germany, as well as to the Czech Sudetendeutsche Party of Herr Henlein. Their important position in domestic Czecho-Slovakia politics had been built up since 1918 in the various agricultural and industrial monopolies which they had secured under the agrarian protectionism of the new state. This protectionism, to which we have already referred, was the Achilles' heel of the more democratic parties in the former state, for the monopolies erected behind it by the Agrarians enabled them to assume complete control in 1938. The extent of their control, shared with the Naziphil Hlinka Guard of autonomous Slovakia, can be estimated from the decision of the new Agrarian Prime Minister, Dr Rudolf Beran, to rule the new state for nearly two years after the end of 1938 without normal Parliamentary discussion and procedure. The decree powers were accorded to him and his Cabinet in the middle of December. Thereafter the triumph of the Right-wing Agrarians was complete. As Dr Beran told Parliament at its last sitting, the new Government's foreign policy was simply to maintain the closest and most sympathetic relations with the Third Reich; and as this was already even more evidently the policy of the Slovaks and Ruthenians in the Central Government German political influence in Prague was, at least for some time to come, secured. If ever it were threatened the economic stranglehold on the new state could be exercised by Germany; the new frontiers could not be defended, so that the proud Czech army could play virtually no anti-German political *rôle* in the new state; and, finally, the Reich had command of the chief communications both inside and out of Czecho-Slovakia. By a judicious combination of German pressures on Poland

and Hungary Czecho-Slovakia might be politically, economically, and militarily immobilized.

Moreover, it gradually became apparent after Munich that the new state was not only being cast for, but actually made to play, a diplomatic *rôle* in the execution of the Reich's eastern and south-eastern policy. We shall see later how the German plans for an ' eastward push ' developed. But here we must emphasize the importance to Germany of the new Czecho-Slovakia in the execution of that policy. The few hundred thousand Ukrainians left in rump Ruthenia served Germany as a base for propagating the idea of an independent but Germanophil Ukrainian state, embodying all of the 45,000,000–50,000,000 Ukrainians living in Poland, Russia, Ruthenia, Rumania—and perhaps those of Hungary as well. Because Poland had precipitately annexed the rich and strategic Teschen-Bohumin region of Czecho-Slovakia when the former state was *in extremis*, all the remaining Czecho-Slovak peoples were incensed against Poland. Accordingly any German plan to dismember Poland could be reliably executed with Czecho-Slovakia's willing assistance. Such aid would naturally involve the use by German troops of all the new state's railways, the new German-planned strategic roads, and the entire terrain of Czecho-Slovakia as far down the map as the junction of Poland with Rumania—which is precisely the region where all the Ruthenians and their Ukrainian brothers in the other countries meet. The significance of Slovak and Ruthenian autonomy to the Reich is evidenced by two events between the second and third weeks of December 1938. The Ruthenian

Ministers of Justice and Propaganda flew to Berlin for a conference there; it was not reported why they went, or why they did not confer in the capital of their federal state—Prague. Secondly, one of the most extreme Slovak autonomists, M. Tuka, who had been in prison for activities dangerous to the Czech state, made a speech in the Slovak capital before M. Tiso, the Slovak Prime Minister, in which he was reported (but not in Czech newspapers) to have demanded complete independence for Slovakia. "Autonomy," he said, "is not enough." Clearly, the erection of small independent states such as Bohemia-Moravia, Slovakia, and Ruthenia would further strengthen Germany's domination of Central Europe, and powerfully advance her "forward policy" in this and other areas.

On the other hand, if these be signs of German domination over the new state it would be idle to pretend that the 7,000,000 Czechs—a hardy, frugal, acutely nation-conscious and collective-minded folk—have fallen head over heels in love with their new master. Their bitterness towards the democracies of the west is understandable. That it should redound to German advantage for the present is natural. They have been forced once more to fall in with German plans, to live again "in the belly of Germany," as they lived in the belly of former Austria. But they are not easy to digest, as the Austrians found four centuries after having swallowed them. They are a small people, like the ants; but they go forth in bands. Like another small folk, the conies, they can scratch homes out of the rock. As long as an uneasy peace, a peace for which they have been sacrificed, endures they will work in resigned and patient collaboration with the vast Third Reich. But let that Reich, like the Austrian Empire before it, plunge into a European war, and the possession of Czech souls and Czech territory may once more become a grave liability. The same is not quite as true of the 3,000,000 Slovaks. They might go hand in hand with the 11,000,000 Magyars who ruled them before the War. But they too may not take long to throw off the temporary ebullience generated by the heady wine of national independence.

For the immediate future scarcely any other prospect is placed before Czecho-Slovakia than utter compliance with German behests. That does not mean to say that other countries, especially Britain and France, should not do all in their power to keep the spirit of Czech nationalism alive. Quite the contrary. But for the foreseeable future Britain and France must not forget the political shade composition of the Government of M. Beran and his fellow-oligarchs. The Western Powers would do well not to place loans at the unfettered disposal and discretionary uses of that Government—a Government which to-day rules over a shadowy federal state, but to-morrow may only be ruling over a rump Bohemia. In this context it is worth recalling that there were rumours of a complete customs and currency union between Germany and Czecho-Slovakia in November 1938.

That the new state needs money and trade is obvious. A country does not lose overnight, at the behest of its friends, all its defences, a third of its population, and half its economic resources without needing funds for its redressment. After all, the frontier defences of former Czecho-Slovakia cost £80,000,000 in four years, and were presented, together with all ' installations,' to Germany. And the new state had at the end of December 1938 125,000 Czech refugees alone to succour, come from the annexed regions without property or money.

Accordingly, if foreign or international aid, financial or commercial, is to be granted to Czecho-Slovakia it should be most carefully devised and accorded, so that the new state is not used by the Third Reich as a beggar's monkey to excite sympathetic charity, or as a secret conduit for money and materials whose other outlet is in the Reich. The negotiations for the disposal of the £5,000,000 balance of the original £10,000,000 granted to the new state by the British Government after Munich showed how difficult it will be in future to secure some control over the uses to which foreign funds are put by any Government of the new state. It would seem that, if the Czech authorities (as they do) require another £20,000,000 or £30,000,000 from abroad for their country's economic redressment, they should understand the reason why the lenders, or even outright donors, still want some control over the expenditure of such sums.

It is not that no one sympathizes with Czecho-Slovakia. It is that, in the terrible plight into which she was forced, even she herself may not be permitted to benefit as fully as she otherwise might from such economic aid—unless her helpers direct and dispense the aid on the spot. Sterling and raw materials are badly needed by Czecho-Slovakia's dominant neighbour, to whom, in all conscience, enough has already been accorded. Without some foreign-directed or international institution in Prague, foreign helpers cannot rely on Czech assurances—not because of Czech bad faith, but because of the vulnerability of Czecho-Slovakia to German *force majeure*. Before that force, as we now realize, the best of good faith can crumble. To strengthen resistance to that force is both the duty and the interest of the Western Powers. But if it be attempted by granting Czecho-Slovakia direct doles they will not be allowed to be spent at her own discretion; and only the *force majeure* will be stronger.

(iii) *Hungary in the Toils*

During the crisis over Czecho-Slovakia the Hungarian Regent, Admiral Horthy, the Prime Minister (formerly Governor of the National Bank), Dr Béla Imrédy, the Foreign Minister, M. de Kánya, and certain of the military staff went to Berchtesgaden to visit Herr Hitler and the Nazi chiefs. On the evening of their return it was announced in Budapest that Hungary was ready to go to " the last extremity " in thwarting any Czecho-Slovak settlement which satisfied only one of the countries preferring claims against Czecho-Slovak territory.

At this time (September 20, 1938) the autumn manœuvres of the Hungarian Army were taking place along the borders of Hungary, Slovakia, and Ruthenia. The next day, the 21st, there was a monster demonstration by Hungarian revisionists in the Liberty Square at Budapest, demanding an assault on Slovakia, in which shouts of

"Long live Hitler! " "Long live Mussolini! " "Long live Imrédy! " "Down with Slovakia! " were heard. For a week before Munich, and for nearly six weeks after it, a strong force of Hungarian irregulars, the so-called 'volunteer' brigade, was encamped and in operation along the Slovak-Ruthene-Hungarian border. They were armed, but had no special uniforms. Their task was to paralyse Slovakia and Ruthenia by smuggling themselves across the frontier at night and then carrying on propaganda and sabotage, with money and other explosive material, behind the uncertain Czecho-Slovak lines. The aim was, of course, to secure most of Slovakia and all of Ruthenia for Hungary, to permit Hungary to join Poland in a *bloc* round Germany's eastern and south-eastern borders. Italy and Jugoslavia were also fore-warned and had given the plan their blessing; so that, once Czecho-Slovakia had been dismembered, the Polish-Hungarian-Jugoslavian-Italian *bloc* would in effect turn out to be a *cordon sanitaire* right round the Third Reich, preventing further expansion to the east or south-east, and protecting all four countries' immediate interests.

This plan was completely scotched by the German Foreign Office, Herr von Ribbentrop, and the Reich-swehr. The two former put stern diplomatic pressure on Budapest, Belgrade, and Rome. The latter warned the Czech military authorities, aided them to rush troops into Slovakia and Ruthenia, and gave an undertaking that the Reichswehr itself would attack Poland and wrest back Teschen-Bohumin if the Polish irregulars (in concert with the Hungarian volunteers) seriously attacked

Ruthenia or Slovakia. Hence the sudden German transfer of three army corps to the Polish frontier already
referred to.

These events were of singular importance to Hungary.
That small neighbour of Greater Germany, disarmed in
comparison with the surrounding three Little Entente
states (Czecho-Slovakia, Rumania, and Jugoslavia), dependent on former Germany and Austria for almost one-
half of its agricultural exports, allied with Italy since
1925, intensely bitter about the dismemberment of its
former territory under the Treaty of Trianon, could do
nothing else but line up with any Powers who promised
it revision of its frontiers. For twenty years every sort of
Hungarian Government had dinned the slogan into Hungarian and all other ears, " Justice for Hungary! " The
crisis over Czecho-Slovakia occurred when Hungarian
politics themselves were abnormally complicated. The
long rule of Count Bethlen as Prime Minister was ended
by his resignation in 1931, at the height of the economic
storm which wrought such havoc in Hungary and all
South-east Europe.

After him, while Germany and Italy went from strength
to strength in Europe, a succession of Hungarian Prime
Ministers—Count Károlyi, General Gömbös, and M.
Darányi—found that popular feeling among the proud,
headstrong, and propaganda-fed masses was turning
more and more towards the Right. This occurred
in a country which had undergone Béla Kun's Communism for six months after the war, and was therefore
consistently Rightward disposed ever since. The net
result was that the Government Coalition Party was

continually finding itself caught between outspoken Hungarian Fascists on its Right (who were shown to be in active collaboration with Fascismo and the Nazi Party) and a powerful Magyar minority, composed of Liberals and the noblest aristocrats in the land, on its Left. Neither Socialism nor Communism existed in this setting. The Government *bloc* for five years tried to take the wind out of the Hungarian Nazis' sails by adopting most of their programme—anti-Semitism, break-up of the big entailed estates of the aristocrats (hence the rather peculiar appearance of the great Hungarian aristocrats on the *Left* of the Government!), reduction of mortgage debts, lowering of interest rates, etc. But the Fascists made more headway among the peasants, especially the million landless agricultural labourers and their dependants, by always promising more than the Government. They also made headway in the towns and big cities by their more extreme anti-Semitism. Accordingly the Government of M. Darányi, up to its collapse in May 1938, found that Hungarians more to its Right and more to its Left were gaining ground at its expense.

Dr Imrédy, a former Finance Minister, was brought into the Darányi Cabinet in its last stages to carry out his ambitious Five-year Plan for the economic redressment of the country. This Plan is for the raising of 1,000,000,000 pengö—600,000,000 by capital levy on big business and the big landlords, 400,000,000 by loan—for expenditure on rearmament and public works. When it became obvious that M. Darányi was losing grip, was not stemming the onrush of the Hungarian Fascists and their foreign associates towards complete control of Hungary's destinies, there was a revolt inside the Darányi Cabinet. The Regent is said to have intervened and stated the alternatives very bluntly to M. Darányi; and the latter resigned.

Dr Imrédy had thus only been Prime Minister for four months when the Czecho-Slovak crisis broke on Europe. In that time he had carried forward the anti-Semitic programme launched by his predecessor, and had even intensified it. Big Jewish businesses were either being Magyarized or expropriated. The Hungarian Fascists were held in check, largely owing to the Regent's and Prime Minister's natural desire to rule unmolested. But the Czecho-Slovak crisis compelled both Regent and Prime Minister to revise their attitudes to the German and Hungarian Nazis. For one thing, they could not, after two decades of sacred propaganda for revisionism, stand out in front of their people against a German offer to secure revision on their behalf. For another, if Germany gained the Sudetenland and Hungary gained nothing—worse, if Poland and Germany gained while Hungary gained nothing — the Hungarian Fascists, doubtless aided by the Nazis, would have pilloried Regent and Prime Minister as traitors and swept them into the gutter. Magyar emotions can be quickly roused to violence.

The position of the Hungarian Regent, Prime Minister, and Foreign Minister was rendered even more uncomfortable since, in the beginning of August, they had all been the guests of the German Government in Berlin and Kiel. At that time M. de Kánya, the old and very shrewd Foreign Minister who had been for many years a trusty servant of Franz Josef in the Vienna Ballhausplatz, and who therefore knew well what had really happened when Austria was annexed in the previous March, was credited with having stoutly resisted Nazi demands for a customs union and military alliance between the Reich and Hungary. More, he apparently carried Dr Imrédy and Admiral Horthy with him. Consequently the delicate situation in which all three Hungarian leaders found themselves on the eve of Munich may be appreciated.

In the event, Hungary did not obtain Ruthenia and Slovakia; the Italians were compelled to desert Hungary's cause, owing to their own greater dependence on the expanded Reich; and Dr Imrédy was compelled to " drop the pilot," the aged and astute Foreign Minister. In M. de Kánya's place was put one of the permanent heads of the Foreign Office, Count Csáky, who was almost immediately (December 1938) summoned to Berlin.

Meanwhile after Munich the anti-Semitic legislation and measures of the Hungarian Government were given a new twist: the land-reform scheme was pressed forward against the big landlords' interests; and the capital levy and loans of the Five-year Plan, drawn up by the Prime Minister, were inaugurated. But Hungary's highly protected industries, though they have gained a new market in the 900,000 agrarian consumers taken from Czecho-Slovakia, depend on imported raw materials; and these materials are paid for by exports of agricultural produce in the main. Hungary, however, is dependent on the Reich market for almost one-half of her exports; and, apart from bauxite and tanning materials, these exports are all agricultural produce. The Reich obviously cannot supply Hungary with the raw materials of industry when it needs all it can get for German industrial needs. Consequently the German half of Hungary's exports is paid for by German manufactures, contracts for works, and—if report be true—repatriation (via the German financial authorities) of some of Hungary's bonded indebtedness to foreigners. Yet all this does not solve Hungary's basic economic problem: how to develop her home industries alongside her agricultural exports, half of which do not bring in any industrial raw material.

Accordingly Dr Imrédy, being an exceptionally able economist and Governor of the National Bank, may decide—may be compelled by Germany's economic predominance to decide—to limit Hungarian home industry to the production of those manufactures that Germany does not want to supply, and to take all other *manufactured* goods from Germany in payment for Hungary's agricultural exports. The country cannot become other than an exporter of agricultural produce in the main. But if it is to buy all its industrial raw materials from other countries than the Reich then it must also export to those countries almost as much agricultural produce as it does to Germany. Thus Hungarian politics and diplomacy are not likely, for the foreseeable future, to be conducted easily and willingly on German behalf. For Hungary can only live, and the hold of Imrédy on the country can therefore only be secure, as long as one of two things is granted. Either the Reich must make itself responsible for meeting all Hungary's needs and taking all her produce—that is, the Hungarian economy, and therefore the state itself, must be utterly incorporated in, or associated with, the Reich's economy—or, secondly, in order to maintain the German hold on at least one-half of Hungary's exports, Hungary must be allowed to trade with the rest of the world to meet her needs of raw materials. The second alternative virtually rules out any possibility of integrating the Hungarian economic system with that of the Reich.

Apart from these economic considerations, Hungarians are not in love with the Nazis. The Magyars fought the Austrians in the middle of last century, and thereafter gained the right to rule, from Budapest, the larger part of the Habsburg dominions. The foundering of Austria in March 1938 brought Prussian rule to Vienna as well as to the confines of Hungary. The dismemberment of the Hungarians' " one foe, one hate," Czecho-Slovakia, within six months unloosed acute mistrust in every Magyar breast save those of the Hungarian Fascists. The latter are a very small minority of the proud, independent, individualistic Magyar folk. Their influence is least strong in the Army—which has always been a strong political cement in Hungary—and Nazi demands are more likely to be made direct to the Government than indirectly by trying to overthrow it.

There is no people in Europe as strongly individualistic as the Hungarian, and the stratification of Hungary's social system is as like that of England as the Hungarian Constitution and limited monarchy is like the English equivalents. (Perhaps that is why the English and Hungarian versions of ' democracy '—less essentially democratic than those of other liberal *régimes* in Europe—have been more successful than those of the German Weimar Republic, France, Czecho-Slovakia, Belgium. For both England and Hungary, with their vestigial aristocracy, their rigidly defined class and caste barriers which every one voluntarily respects, thereby gain in national cohesion.) In Hungary too, then, the enlarged Third Reich finds, as in rump Czecho-Slovakia, another small folk on its present periphery—a people not willing to be tyrannized; a grudging collaborator in peace, but a formidable blackmailer and rebel in time of war. To secure Hungary's wheat, cattle, poultry, fruit, in peace-time, when other countries leave to the Reich a free field there, is easy. To ensure increased supplies of these things in war-time, and to ensure that over 10,000,000 Magyars will in fact march with Germany, may require an occupation of the centre of the Danubian Basin which will be extremely costly—as costly in money as it will assuredly be in men.

Hungary to-day has no defences against Germany; she is the only truly non-Slav neighbour on Germany's eastern or south-eastern borders; she might easily be made to do German bidding, might easily be bankrupted or overrun if she did not. But once she has done German bidding to regain her Magyar souls and territories from Rumania and Jugoslavia, once she has Magyar lands and a united or undiluted Magyar population, she may prove to be a formidable and intractable neighbour. In this connexion we do well to recall that when Magyar overlords and Slav or Ruman subjects were at daggers drawn before the breakdown of the Habsburg monarchy there was no common enemy. Russia, which the Teutonic Austrians in Vienna most feared, was the friend and Great Father of all Austria-Hungary's Slavs. To-day it might be neither surprising nor difficult for Magyar and Slav in South-eastern Europe to put their heads, their trade, their hands, together. And secretly the Italians might be glad to see that happen.

One thing alone is sure: the Hungarians may be prepared in future, as in the recent past, to do a little military freebooting on their own revisionist account; but they loathe and fear the prospect revealed, so soon after their 1918 tragedy, of being once again embroiled in a general European war between the Great Powers. They are a small, poor, defenceless, but proud and defiant people. Their national hymn epitomizes the tragedy of their position in history and geography alike: " Lord, remember this people, who have suffered enough in the past to atone for all the future! " As individuals they are the best of friends; as a people, the worst of neighbours. Only one man really got the better of Bismarck, and he was a Magyar—Count Andrássy.

(iv) *Poland : " the Nutcracker Suite "*

Poland after Munich is vitally interested in the destiny of Danubia, for she now holds the Moravian Gap (Teschen-Bohumin) between Northern and Central Europe; and, secondly, the enlarged Third Reich and Czecho-Slovakia are together staking out claims on

Poland, so that the Central and South-east European extension of the Reich takes on vital importance for her. We are familiar with the German, and enforced Italian, baulking of the Polish-Hungarian plan to join their frontiers over Eastern Czecho-Slovakia. Isolated Poland is, therefore, like a nut in the crackers, between Germany and Russia. After the dismemberment of Czecho-Slovakia, in which Poland was quick to share, there can be no southward or south-eastward escape from the nut-crackers.

One of the factors which decided Colonel Beck, Poland's Foreign Minister, to occupy the Teschen-Bohumin area in such haste was that this area could otherwise have fallen to the Third Reich. If Germany held it the knot of important rail and road connexions at Bohumin would have allowed the Moravian Gap, the entry to Galicia and the Polish Ukraine, to have served Germany as a southern corridor into Poland, like the Polish Corridor between Germany proper and East Prussia in the north. The Polish troops which annexed the region proceeded at once to prepare defensive positions against Germany and Czecho-Slovakia. Clearly, the dismemberment of former Czecho-Slovakia, albeit in Poland's immediate favour, rendered Poland's Silesian, Galician, and Ukrainian territories vulnerable to an assault from German Silesia and a German-controlled Czecho-Slovakia.

The importance of Southern Poland lies in its heavy industry, oil deposits, coal- and lignite-mines, as well as in the strategic Silesia-Gdynia railway, already described. Poland's armament and defensive industries have been established in what is known as the 'strategic triangle' which has Warsaw for its apex, Silesia for one foot, and the Ukraine for the other. This south-central region is equidistant from the German and Russian frontiers. It would, so it was thought during the last six years, enable Poland to maintain her 1,500,000 troops in the field even if the Polish Corridor were taken by Germany. On this point there is grave doubt. For Poland, like almost every other state of Europe beyond Germany, depends for industrial output on imported raw materials. Though she has a surplus of all foodstuffs, coal, oil, timber, lead, and zinc, she needs all the more important strategic metals, from iron ore to antimony and molybdenum. Her naval forces cannot guarantee her access to Swedish iron ore, for Germany's fleet can command the Baltic. Consequently Russia's help to Poland in the event of a German-Polish war would be invaluable.

On the other hand, Russian 'help' for Poland still terrifies most Poles, who remember the century of oppression under the Russian Czars, and fear that the Bolsheviks, whom the Poles defeated with French military aid in 1920, would never leave Polish soil once they were on it. (This fear is held in common by Finns, Estonians, Letts, Lithuanians, and Rumanians.) Thus, though Colonel Beck hastened in December 1938 to re-insure Poland with Lithuania and Russia, signing pacts of reconciliation with them in face of German threats, relations between Poland and Russia are always likely to be delicate and unreliable. Such economic agreements between them as that of December 1938, outwardly extremely significant, are not likely to decide military or political policy. For one thing, the Lithuanians were compelled in this recent pact to renounce all claims to their historic city of Vilna, under the more pressing German threat to Memel. For another, both Poles and Russians remembered that before Munich M. Litvinov had sternly threatened Poland with denunciation of the Polish-Soviet Pact of Non-Aggression should Polish troops enter Czech territory. Munich, of course, altered that; but the rancour remained.

Of all states vulnerable to German demands after Munich, Poland and Hungary were the most exposed. They were deprived of their long-planned common frontier. The foreign organization of the Nazi Party, collaborating (as it had done even before the Nazis' advent to power) with the headquarters of the Ukrainian autonomists' movement in Berlin, and working from the now autonomous Ruthenia, was reported to have expended R.M. 5,000,000 in three months on the campaign for an independent Ukrainian state. Here we can examine this plan in greater detail. Ever since the independence of the Ukrainian Republic was destroyed by the military superiority of the Bolsheviks at the end of the last war a Ukrainian autonomists' movement had been located in Berlin. The Nazis, as *Mein Kampf* shows, aimed at creating a Ukrainian state—either as an associated Germanophil republic or as a monarchy under the last of the Romanovs—embodying the Ukrainians of Poland, White Russia, the Ukrainian Soviet Republic, Ruthenia, and Rumania. Such a state would stretch from German Silesia, Slovakia, and Hungary across Polish, Rumanian, and Russian territories almost to the

Volga. The Nazi plan had made this state the vanguard of that German expansion which was to realize the project outlined in *Mein Kampf*: "If we had at our disposal the incalculable wealth and supplies of raw materials in the Ural Mountains and the interminable fertile plains of the Ukraine, for exploitation under National-Socialist leadership, then we would produce and our German people would swim in plenty." A state of nearly 50,000,000 inhabitants, albeit Slavs, might be expected to work in grateful co-operation with the Nazis who had realized its independence for it.

Accordingly, when in December of 1938 the elections in the Memel district led the local Nazi leader to declare that Memel would demand to be reincorporated in Germany, and when the Poles found a large force of the Reichswehr being mobilized on their southern frontier, the danger signals for Poland could not be mistaken. The annexation of Memel-land, at the request of the Memel Germans, would mean that Lithuania lost her chief outlet to the Baltic, through which more than half her trade was carried. On the other hand, though the League of Nations still had nominal charge of Danzig's free status, the League had, at Colonel Beck's request, left the settlement of Danzig's future status to Poland and Germany. If Memel returned to Germany Danzig could not be expected long to remain nominally independent, for the Nazi Party had complete control of the Free City. And once the Danzig question was peremptorily raised by Germany the future of the Corridor would be involved. Thus, finally, not only Lithuania's outlet to the Baltic, but also Poland's only outlet—

Gdynia and the strategic Silesia-Gdynia railway—would be threatened with extinction. Poland and Lithuania were alike in danger of encirclement, by land and sea, from the German side. And if Germany 'rushed' the Corridor, linking up East Prussia with the Fatherland once more, then Poland's western front would be a gigantic salient thrust forward into Germany—another "spearhead in Germany's flank," as the Nazi Press continuously described the former Czecho-Slovakia—destined, in all probability, to incur the same fate as that unhappy country.

These considerations, however, were not the most discomfiting to Poland. Even worse was the Polish domestic problem caused by the sudden—suspiciously sudden—outbreak of Ukrainian autonomists' demands on the Polish Government after Munich. In November and December 1938 the Deputy-Marshal of the Diet, Dr Mudryj, who is also leader of the Ukrainian movement in Poland, outlined a set of demands, embodied in a Bill. These envisaged the creation of an autonomous Polish Ukraine, with its own Diet, its Cabinet forming part of the Polish Central Government, control over its own finances, justice, and education, and a separate military establishment. As Lwów (Lemberg) was selected for the capital, and as the new province's south-western frontier would abut on autonomous Czecho-Slovak Ruthenia, peopled by the same Ukrainian folk, the possibility of German permeation of the new unit was obvious. The Polish Silesian and Galician industrial region would be caught between the Reich proper, Bohemia-Moravia and Slovakia, and Ruthenia. Poland's 'strategic triangle' would be surrounded on the west, south, and east; and if at any time the Danzig and Corridor problems blazed up into an inflammation of Polish-German relations an autonomous Ukrainian province in Eastern and Southern Poland would be an inestimable basis for a German diversion. It was not surprising that the Speaker of the Sejm refused to accept Dr Mudryj's Bill, on the ground that it required an amendment to the Polish Constitution. But the Nazi plan of campaign gained in intensity; and the inevitability of the retrocession of Memel and Danzig loomed as further dangers over Poland's head.

Indeed, at the end of 1938 it was obvious that Colonel Beck's policy of friendship with the Third Reich, a policy which had been bequeathed to him by Marshal Pilsudski and enshrined in the Ten-year Pact of Amity between Poland and Germany in 1934, was becoming severely strained. Inside Poland the rule of the Colonels —the heroes of the last war, as the Legionaries were in Czecho-Slovakia—was still untrammelled. But the peasants amounted to 70 per cent. of the population, and they were largely either in opposition to the Government *bloc* or disfranchised. At the 1938 elections they boycotted the polling-booths; and the pronounced sympathy of Marshal Smigly-Rydz, successor to the old Marshal as Inspector-General of the Forces, with the peasants' claims did not make for unity in the Central Government. An attempt by the new Marshal and his adjutant, Colonel Adam Koc, in 1937 to establish a kind of party-state was defeated by intrigue among the Colonels themselves, who feared they might lose power if the peasants were given a share in administration. At the municipal elections all over Poland in December, the first on a national scale since 1927, the Government *bloc* lost many seats to the Left and Right extremes.

Thus, outwardly a unitary state, Poland after Munich began to experience the first tremors of internal weakness and dissension. To these inward tremors were added threats from abroad of disruption or dismemberment. A country with minorities—Germans, Jews, Ukrainians, and now Czechs—amounting to one-third of her population, and a country so strategically placed, can ill afford enemies, either abroad or of her own household. Poland has both. Her only reliable reinforcements, economic and military, against Germany must come either in a general European war (which would divide Germany's forces), or else, if she is left alone to face Germany in Eastern and Central Europe, from Russia in her rear. It is now quite possible that a race against time will begin—Germany pressing Poland from without and from within, while Colonel Beck strives to overcome Polish mistrust of Russia in time for Poland to face westward. Even then he may call, but the Russians may not come.

It should not be thought that Russia needs to support Poland in a straightforward Polish-German war. The Third Reich does not desire a war with Russia on Polish soil. Such a war would be risky. It might so weaken Germany in the east that all manner of unpleasant events might occur in other sectors, as well as inside the recently enlarged Reich territory. The strategists of the Third Reich, especially those versed in the new art of military economics (*Wehrwirtschaft*), are reported to have urged on Nazi extremists and visionaries the desirability of maintaining a smaller Poland as a buffer-state in the north between the two totalitarian Great Powers of Northern Europe. The Corridor, Danzig, Memel, Polish Silesia, and Galicia—these, joined to the Reich, would repatriate the bulk of Poland's Germans and give Germany the valuable Polish oil-deposits on the northern slopes of the Carpathians. (The acquisition of still greater surpluses of coal and lignite would be a disadvantage, outweighed by the control of large surpluses of foodstuffs, more heavy industries, and badly needed oil supplies.) If a small Poland were retained as a pure Slav state, like the rump of Czecho-Slovakia, Polish people annexed to the Reich would doubtless be made to leave, as the Czech refugees were made to leave the annexed Bohemian territories, becoming a charge on the new state, and thus rendering it more economically dependent on its enlarged neighbour.

The erection of a separate Ukrainian state would serve the same German purpose. It might well be a long time, perhaps five or ten years or more, before the expanding Third Reich felt itself strong enough to use its new vassal states in the east as corridors for an assault on Russia. And in the meantime the Reich might be forced to take military action in another direction. In the latter eventuality the presence of a number of small, independent Slav states from the Baltic down to Rumania might be a sure shield against a possibly aggressive Russia. The smaller such states were the less the possibility that they might coalesce with their great Slav neighbour to the east. The smaller they were the greater their apprehensions might be of the political and economic system of the Soviet Union. Such separatism and such fears might enable the Reich the more easily to control them while it was elsewhere occupied.

(v) *Rumania in Reaction*

Rumania is the Mexico of the Balkans: a beautiful country, rich in fertile lands and minerals, torn asunder by revolt and reaction, and consequently backward in developing its own resources. Like Poland, its minorities are ranged round its periphery. Like Poland, after Munich it finds itself between Russia and Germany; only in the case of Rumania the vanguard of the Third Reich is still engaged in penetrating towards Rumania through Hungary and (more easily) Czecho-Slovak Ruthenia. While the Third Reich ardently desires the wheat and maize fields, the oil deposits, the other minerals of Rumania, Soviet Russia has a common frontier with her from Poland down to the Black Sea, which is Rumania's only reliable connexion with the outside world. The Slavs in the Bukovina and Bessarabia, alongside Russia, are so poor that the Russian *régime* is more attractive to them than it is to any other Slavs in Europe. Hungary is still bent upon the retrocession of Transylvania, in which the 'unredeemed' Magyars and Germans live, surrounded by Rumans; consequently German penetration through Hungary towards Rumania is a real threat, with which any Hungarian Government might temporarily and willingly associate itself. Bulgaria still wants the return of that portion of the Dobrudja taken from her by Rumania after the Second Balkan War in 1913, regained under the German-imposed Treaty of Bucharest in 1917, and ceded in 1919. The Soviet Union, though it was prepared during the Czecho-Slovak crisis in 1938 to barter its renunciation of Bessarabia against Rumanian permission for Russian troops and war material to cross the Bukovina corridor into Czecho-Slovak Ruthenia, has not technically abandoned its pretensions to Bessarabia. Consequently Rumania is exposed to many external threats; and her position is not rendered easier by the realization that all these threats can be reduced to conflicting ambitions, at her expense, on the part of the German-Italian or the Russian systems.

When Rumania collapsed before the arms of the Central Powers in 1917 the Rumanians set fire to their cereals and their oil-wells rather than let them fall into the hands of Germany. Then they acted upon the urgent requests of the Allies. To-day Italy, once among the Allies, is bound hand and foot to the Rome-Berlin Axis; and contact between Rumania and her friends in the west is only possible by the goodwill of Russia and Turkey—the former able and ready to invade Rumania to prevent her resources from falling into Germany's lap, the latter in military control of the Straits since 1937. An Italy hostile to Britain and France could make it difficult for Rumania to oppose German designs and to keep in contact with the west—even if Turkey kept open the Straits—by attempting to block the passage of the Mediterranean half-way. Accordingly

Rumania's position in the event of a general European war is very like that of Poland—one of isolation, apart from Russian aid. And Russian aid is viewed askance by both contiguous states. Whereas, however, Poland might deter Russia from forcibly giving ' aid,' Rumania, with a small army and air force not yet properly equipped by the Czech Skoda contracts and credits, may never be able to deter the Russians from entering her territories.

It is reported that the German authorities have intervened in Prague to stop completion of the Skoda contracts for Rumania, on the ground that these credits for the rearmament of Rumania were a part of the " Beneš policy of collaboration with Bolshevism." If that is so then the geography of Rumania will become a great asset to Russia, for the Rumanians will be unable to stop the Russians from entering as soon as the Third Reich makes a warlike thrust eastward or south-eastward; and Russia can do this quite simply, since the great arc of the Carpathians and Balkans lies between the Rumanian plain and Germany, Hungary, or Ruthenia. The Rumanian oil-wells and fertile lands can be occupied, and the great natural mountain-barrier garrisoned with Russians before any substantial German force can ever think of piercing it. In that case the unhappy Hungarians and Ruthenians might find themselves ' out on a limb,' where the Reichswehr would have to maintain and support them. The extent of such a Russo-Rumanian diversion south-east of Germany and Czecho-Slovakia might be such as to draw off a considerable portion of the Reich's armed forces to prevent yet another crumpling of the south-eastern front. But these operations would be undertaken at fearful cost to the unfortunate Hungarians and Ruthenians.

The important reaction of Rumania to German influence was really begun by King Carol at Easter 1938, when, after trying to rule with the Germanophil Goga Cabinet, he suddenly—and personally—arrested all the leaders of the Fascist Iron Guard. This avowedly Germanophil and Italophil terroristic organization was to some extent imbued with idealism, with a sense of Rumania's obvious need for a national regeneration. The quarrel between the Iron Guard on the one hand and the monarchy and traditional parties on the other arose as a dispute over the leadership of that regeneration. The King was as disillusioned with the corrupt, hand-to-mouth tactics of the older parties as were the Rumanian peasants and the Iron Guard itself. Like the ill-fated Alexander of Jugoslavia, he determined to abolish the existing constitution and instal a personal political *régime*; this he accomplished in March 1938. He rallied round him a group of able young Rumanian administrators and Army officers; and at Easter, acting on information about the Iron Guard's relations with the Nazis and Italian Fascists, he and his *entourage* rounded up the ringleaders. From that moment, however, he became the focus alike of fanatical support and criticism. The monarch was in the political arena, and the monarchy with him. The new Government, headed by the Patriarch, strove to steal much of the Iron Guard's thunder—for example, like Dr Imrédy's Government in Hungary, it sought to secure popular support among the great bulk of the population, the peasantry, by unleashing anti-Semitic measures—without seeming to be illiberal or reactionary. The task was beyond its powers. The more firmly the King governed the farther underground went the Iron Guard. After Munich, as in Poland, the clandestine activities of the local agents of the Nazi Party flared out in political assassinations—like the murder of the Rumanian Prime Minister, M. Duca, by Iron Guards in 1934.

The plan miscarried. It was scheduled for execution during the latter half of November 1938, just after King Carol left on his visit to London and Berlin. It was to present him on his return with a Fascist Government, holding all the key positions in Rumania. The King's trusted friends in the Army discovered all details; and as soon as the monarch returned a clean sweep of the Iron Guard throughout the country was ordered. In this operation the leaders of the Iron Guard were shot by the authorities, so it is reported, while attempting to escape from their escort. The chagrin in Germany was expressed in a vitriolic outburst in the German newspapers under Dr Goebbel's control.

But the domestic situation in Rumania was not calm after this storm. For one thing, King Carol had had talks with Field-Marshal Goering and Herr Hitler while he was in Germany. He had also tried to secure a loan and commercial concessions from the British authorities while he was in London—according to report, without success. The fact that Germany after Munich would be taking more of Rumania's oil, cereals, and minerals became known in December; and the German-Rumanian trade talks are said to have broached the possibility of Rumania's guaranteeing the Reich 40 per cent. of her total exports—that is, an increase over the 1937 figure of about one-half. As these talks were held in Bucharest after the clean-up of the Iron Guard, and as an increase in Germany's imports from Rumania could only take place in the much-needed cereals, oil, and timber, many observers began to ask themselves if King Carol had merely yielded to German pressure on condition that he, and no other, should be in control of Rumania's destinies. If so the liquidation of the Iron Guard's leaders might, of course, be accepted by German authorities as a regrettable price, but one over which no haggling could be permitted. In that case, the virulent German Press campaign against the Rumanian monarch-dictator might have to be written off as (a) a vent for the feelings of the Iron Guard's associates among the Nazi extremists, or (b) a pre-arranged gesture to satisfy Nazi indignation in Germany, or (c) a deliberate pulling of wool over the eyes of the outside world. In any case, these hypotheses, though naturally aroused by the irreconcilable nature of German and Rumanian statements in censored publications, do not bring us nearer the truth. The truth, indeed, seems to be that King Carol is trying to ensure the integrity of his country and the reversion of his throne to Crown Prince Michael; and that in dealing with desperate men at home and abroad he has had recourse to desperate methods.

Rumania cannot remain unaffected by German diplomatic measures against Poland and Hungary. King Carol himself refused to aid and abet Colonel Beck on October 18, 1938, when the Polish Foreign Minister flew to visit him to secure Rumanian support for the joint Polish-Hungarian plan for a common frontier; and the reason was obvious. Despite King Carol's desire to avoid the Nazi Satan, he did not wish to invoke the Hungarian Beelzebub for the task. Once he had supported Hungary in obtaining a common frontier over Ruthenia with Poland he would have been faced with Hungarian demands for the cession of Transylvania; and Germany would have been supporting an aggrandized Hungary. Moreover, after Munich Rumania could still hope that the next German drive would be at Polish expense. Even so, as we have seen, the ultimate threat to Transylvania and the Bukovina remains; for the stronger Germany becomes the greater the possibility that an independent Ukrainian state will be erected partly at Rumanian expense, and the greater the domination of Hungary by the Reich. In exchange for that domination the Reich, while erecting the Ukrainian state or after doing so, can threaten to secure Transylvania for Hungary. The omens for Rumania are in no way bright.

(vi) *Jugoslavia and the Axis*

Yet another example of a Slav state caught in the pincers is Jugoslavia. Bordering on Germany and Italy in her northern mountain fastness, she faces Italy across the Adriatic, where her substantial seaborne commerce finds its way out to the world's markets. In her rear revisionist Hungary, with eyes on the rich wheatfields of the Backa district, taken from Hungary after the last war, may at any moment be used as a jumping-off spot by German strategists. The common interests of Germany and Italy after the annexation of Austria demand the immobilization of Jugoslavia, on both their flanks. Moreover, the Reich's increased import requirements may urge both Germany and Italy to secure the position of Trieste by a slight amputation of Jugoslav territory in the north, which would give both of them another purely Italo-German railway connexion between Central Europe and the Mediterranean.

The triune Kingdom of Serbs, Croats, and Slovenes has never solved the same problem which vexed Czecho-Slovakia and still vexes Poland; and all of them are Slav states. That problem, of course, is the reconciliation of national self-determination, by which all three states came into being after 1918, with their constituent Slav peoples' demands for autonomy inside each state. Thus, while former Czecho-Slovakia solved the problem of her disparate Slav elements, she could not solve it for the Germans and Magyars when they became anvils on which foreign Powers beat out their own policies. Poland has never solved it for her (Slav) Ukrainians. Jugoslavia, compounded of three big Slav elements, has never solved it for the Croats and Slovenes—to say nothing of her (non-Slav) Magyar minority. Accordingly party politics in the triune Kingdom have ever since its foundation been more the reflection of family quarrels than of economic, class, or ideological differentiation.

Jugoslavia's domestic politics dissolved on the assassination of King Alexander at Marseilles in 1934 into a welter of personal ambitions, jealousies, and rival authoritarianisms. The Regency, headed by Prince Paul, attempted to hold the country's domestic life together by entrusting the conduct of affairs to the Serb Dr Stoyadinovitch as Prime Minister, whose adjutant was the Slovene Father Koroshetz, Minister of the Interior. The clamant Croats, under a cloud since the murder of the King, remained in opposition; but they received gradually support from dissident Serbs. The cause of this surprising development was the equivocal foreign policy followed by Dr Stoyadinovitch. The Prime Minister's internal *régime* became steadily more and more authoritarian; the organs of public opinion, together with free speech and public meetings, were muzzled; and all this was done in an effort to draw Jugoslavia into peaceful collaboration with the two Axis Powers, from whom she had most to fear.

To this end Dr Stoyadinovitch had to talk with one voice to the Czecho-Slovak and Rumanian statesman, his associates in the Little Entente; with another voice he tried to woo Italy and Germany. His own people grew more and more restive; and as the pressure on their Czecho-Slovak cousins succeeded to the violent annexation of Austria the Serbs, Croats, and Slovenes tended to reach a kind of unity in resentment against Dr Stoyadinovitch. All Jugoslavs in their ' Sokols '—the semi-political, democratic, nationalistic formations of Slavs for athletic prowess—insisted, against the Prime Minister's wish, on sending a national contingent to the Sokol festival at Prague in July 1938. Demonstrations in favour of France and Czecho-Slovakia took place on the slightest pretext, and the police were employed to clear the streets of many a Jugoslav city. Tension was not allayed by the attempt of the Prime Minister in 1937 to drive through Parliament a concordat with the Roman Catholic Church. This uncovered the deep religious divisions between Orthodox Serbs and Catholic Croats and Slovenes, while the peculiar behaviour of the Austrian Catholic hierarchy in hastily Heil-ing Hitler after the annexation of Austria drove the Catholic Jugo-slav element back upon Belgrade again. Thus the dissident Serbs who feared that Dr Stoyadinovitch was aiming at personal dictatorship, among whom were General Zhivkovitch and a former Prime Minister, M. Yevtitch, were able to make common cause with the Croat autonomists.

Throughout Jugoslavia there was general resentment at the increase of authoritarianism; and voices were raised to point out that the Regent, Prince Paul, in his natural antipathy to Left-wing tendencies (he is related to the ill-fated Romanovs' house) was running a dangerous risk in allowing his Prime Minister to revolve about the Rome-Berlin Axis. The risk was, of course, lest Germany support Hungary in demanding the Backa again—and perhaps other pre-War regions of Hungary —and combine with Italy to ' prune ' Jugoslav territory in the north.

On the other hand, after Munich Dr Stoyadinovitch was quick to see that Czecho-Slovakia's fate contained a moral for his own countrymen. He called a General Election for December, and (not without due Balkan manipulation) secured the handsome victory that normally graces the Balkan Government in power at election time. This was claimed as an endorsement of his policy of conciliation with Italy and Germany. There, however, as in Poland and Rumania, the matter cannot rest. Before the elections Dr Matchek, the Croat autonomists' leader (and the elections showed that there are virtually no other Croats but autonomists) openly demanded autonomy within the state, a Diet, and a federal Jugo-slavia. The 4,000,000 Croats and Slovenes, mainly Roman Catholic, can always be outvoted under a central-ized political system, which automatically gives the Serbs the dominant *rôle* at elections and in the administration. But such a system has always resulted in uneasy domestic relations; and for the foreseeable future it contains the seeds of dissension within itself—seeds which the two Axis Powers are assiduously tending. Reference to these internal dangers was made by British authorities when Prince Paul visited London at the beginning of Decem-ber 1938. But the aftermath of Munich was to convince both the Regent and his Prime Minister of the necessity for an understanding with the Axis Powers.

Dr Stoyadinovitch had been indefatigable in improv-ing relations between the Balkan Entente (Turkey, Greece, Rumania, and Jugoslavia) and the defeated Central Power in their midst—Bulgaria. By a Treaty of Amity in January of 1937 Jugoslavia went a long way towards making Bulgaria a member of the Balkan Entente, which the latter Power had not been invited to join by reason of her revisionist claims against Greece and Rumania. This gave Dr Stoyadinovitch himself a position of crucial importance within the Entente, for Jugoslavia's position was really that of an intermediary between the entire Entente and Bulgaria. It also provided him with a shield against any extreme demands upon Jugoslavia by Italy, for Italy's influence upon Bulgaria had declined while Jugoslavia's had been increasing. This acquisition of strength by Jugoslavia in the Balkan arena had a certain value, since the Jugoslav-Italian Pact of March 1937 (two months after the Jugoslav-Bulgarian Pact) was very unpopular among Jugoslavs themselves, who could not easily forget the 400,000 Slovenes and Croats incorporated in Italy after the War.

Jugoslavia's foreign trade has undergone a sudden redirection in recent years. Whereas in 1929 she sent 25 per cent. of her total exports to Italy, and took only 11 per cent. of her imports from that country, in 1937 the percentages were 9 and 8 respectively, mainly owing to the League's economic sanctions against Italy in 1935–36. This was one of the relations to be improved under the Italo-Jugoslav Pact of March 1937, but it has not substantially improved, for one of the reasons that the trade originally declined. Italy's currency and exchange-controls were imposed after 1929, as the outcome of her transition from a peace-time to a war-time economy. Therewith her needs of strategic raw materials became paramount. She could not supply Jugoslavia with the materials Jugoslavia needed, and Jugoslavia produced for herself most of the products which Italy could export. Accordingly Jugoslavia's exports to Italy were curtailed to a level at which her imports from Italy, which Jugoslavia really required, could exactly offset them. Meanwhile Jugoslavia's trade with Germany and Austria increased until, after the annexation of Austria by Germany, the same difficulty emerged again. Both Italy and the enlarged Reich badly need Jugoslavia's flax, hemp, timber, iron ore, copper, lead, zinc, bauxite, chrome ore, pyrites, cereals, cattle, meat, and dairy products.

Jugoslavia is an ideal repository of mineral and food resources. But whereas the Reich has shown itself prepared to liquidate Jugoslavia's past blocked balances—by exporting more manufactures or undertaking large-scale contracts, to a total value about 10 per cent. above the current level of Jugoslav exports to Germany—Italy's financial and trading position has been strained so much that she cannot restore her trade with Jugoslavia. Incidentally, it may here be mentioned that Jugoslavia's larger imports from the Greater Reich do not indicate that she is becoming indebted to the Reich, but that she is unfreezing the Reichsmark proceeds of her heavier exports to Germany in former years. Briefly, the triune Kingdom in 1938 was conducting about one-half of its foreign trade with the Greater Reich (including the Sudetenland), Italy, and the remnant of Czecho-Slovakia. Yet the Jugoslav authorities felt themselves strong enough, knowing the Reich's and Italy's urgent needs, to insist, when Dr Funk's delegation visited Belgrade after Munich, on equalizing Jugoslav imports from Germany with exports to Germany.

Thus, Jugoslavia has both a political and an economic possibility of playing one Axis partner against the other. The supreme risk of this position is that both partners may act in concert against Jugoslavia, politically as well as economically. Then it would be a grim outlook for Jugoslavia.

(vii) *The Balkan Peninsula*

Brief mention must be made of the remaining countries in the Balkan peninsula—Bulgaria, Greece, and Turkey. Albania is, politically and economically, an extension of Italy upon the Balkan mainland.

King Boris of Bulgaria has been forced, unwillingly, to take upon his shoulders the unenviable task assumed by the late King Alexander of Jugoslavia and more recently by King Carol of Rumania. Once the vexed question of the Macedonian minority had been settled between Jugoslavia and Bulgaria their relations improved; but domestic politics in Bulgaria went from bad to worse. There was not much violence in the process; but the full force of the economic slump was felt by this small country, and its virtual dependence on exports of tobacco, wheat, and dairy produce—all three commodities fell fast and far in price—presented successive Governments with acute problems. It is almost entirely, as its exports indicate, a peasant country; consequently the Third Reich was able to contract for a higher percentage of its export trade than in any other country. In 1936, indeed, just under 60 per cent. of Bulgaria's total foreign trade was with the Germany of that year, compared with under 25 per cent. in 1929. In 1938 it is calculated that about the same percentage as in 1936 will be taken by the Greater Reich—that is, 60 per cent. As in the case of Jugoslavia, imports from the Reich have risen sharply, in order, after a 'lag' of about one year between the sets of figures, to unfreeze the Bulgarian blocked balances of Reichsmarks which piled up as a result of formerly heavier exports from Bulgaria to Germany.

King Boris and his Prime Minister, M. Kiosséivanov, have now to meet increased agitation in Bulgaria for revision of Bulgaria's frontiers with Rumania and Greece. The claim against Rumania is for the Southern Dobrudja, already mentioned. The claim against Greece is the long-standing demand for an outlet to the Ægean Sea, which, it is asserted, Greece promised to give Bulgaria after the War. The Greeks were only prepared to assign the use of a corridor to Dedeagatch, on the Ægean, and the use of the port itself. They refused to cede the corridor and port. While the terrorist activities against Jugoslavia and Greece of the Macedonian *comitadjis* under Mihailov have been stamped out, these claims remain.

After Munich the revisionist demands flared up in Bulgaria as much as they did in her late ally among the Central Powers, Hungary. In November and December 1938 there were violent street demonstrations in Sofia against the Kiosséivanov Government for its ' docility ' towards the Greeks and Rumanians, Bulgaria's recent associates in the Bulkan Entente, into which unofficial association she has been brought by her closer relations with the Government of Dr Stoyadinovitch in Jugoslavia. Nevertheless, if Central Europe and the Balkans were once more plunged into war it is difficult to see how a small, weak, and poverty-stricken Bulgaria could take the war-path against such relatively strong neighbours as Jugoslavia, Rumania, Turkey, and Greece— especially as all these are allies in the Balkan Entente, one of the secret ' understandings ' of which provides for a common front against any attempt at forcible frontier-revision by Bulgaria, directed against any one of them. Bulgaria, it must be remembered, is surrounded on land by the four partners of the Balkan Entente; and Rumania controls the outlet of the Danube into the Black Sea.

Greece herself has successfully settled her long and embittered disputes with Turkey and Jugoslavia. The Greek monarchy was in abeyance between 1923 and 1935, when King George II was recalled; but administration has since come under the virtual control of General John Metaxas, whose position is that of Dr Salazar in Portugal—a political and economic dictator. The Greeks, notwithstanding their (not wholly popular) dictatorship, have been consistent in their distrust of Italy and Germany—of the former owing to Italian naval measures in the Ægean and control of the Dodecanese islands, of the latter because of German influence in Bulgaria. This has not, however, for obvious reasons, prevented the Greater Reich's share of Greek foreign trade (imports and exports together) from rising between 1929 and 1938 from about 16 per cent. to about $33\frac{1}{3}$ per cent. Greek tobacco, hides, raisins, iron ore, pyrites, chrome ore, and bauxite figure largely among Germany's and Italy's needs. On the other hand, Greek trade with Italy, like the Jugoslav and Bulgarian trade with Italy, slumped abruptly after the sanctions episode. Moreover, in 1937 Britain accounted for nearly 10 per cent. of total Greek foreign trade. France, the United States, and Britain together accounted for 25 per cent. of Greece's foreign trade as a whole in that year, whereas Italy accounted for only 5 per cent. and Germany (without Austria) for 27 per cent. The importance of British and French trade with Greece and Turkey can best be realized by looking at the map. Greece and Turkey, whose mutual relations have been so improved as to withstand the European shocks of recent years, virtually enclose the Ægean Sea, with its Italian naval and air bases, and control the entry into, and exit from, the Danube and Black Sea *via* the Straits. Their geographical, military, and economic positions are, therefore, of crucial importance to all the countries of the Danubian Basin, as well as to Russia.

Turkey's strategic importance is, moreover, enhanced by her control of the landward connexion between Europe and Asia Minor, her railways leading to Palestine, Egypt, and Iraq—though the projected Scutari-Aleppo-Mosul-Bagdad-Basra railway is not yet completed as a ' through ' line. Turkey for many years has been in close relations with the Soviet Union, on whose economic development President Kemal Atatürk largely modelled that of his own republic. This relationship too has stood the test of time—which is remarkable, in that the two countries might have been expected to have conflicts of interest in the Black Sea and the Caucasian Isthmus—and the death of the Atatürk on November 10, 1938, is not expected to change Turko-Soviet relations, since the former Prime Minister, General Ismet Inönü, schooled by the late President, was unanimously elected President on November 11 by the Kamutay (National Assembly).

Despite the large share of Turkey's total foreign trade taken by the Soviet Union, Germany increased her share from about 14 per cent. in 1929 to about 35 per cent. in 1937; and in 1938 the share of the enlarged Third Reich is estimated to reach about 40 per cent. Owing to the high prices (in Turkish currency) offered by Germany for Turkish products, more and more of these products were earmarked for export through the 'clearing' office to Germany; and at the beginning of 1937 the Turkish authorities called a halt to the process, finding that Germany owed Turkey upward of £T3,000,000. Partly to 'unfreeze' this balance standing to their credit in Germany, the Turkish authorities accepted long-term credits from Germany for armaments and public works. The rest of this blocked balance is understood to have been liquidated, or arranged for gradual liquidation, in the ten-year German 'credit' of R.M.150,000,000 to Turkey, made by Dr Funk in Angora during October 1938 (see p. 168). Such is the nature of the 'credits' from the Reich.

Meanwhile Turkey had, in May 1938, negotiated a credit of £16,000,000 from the British Government for naval and other armaments, as well as industrial equipment. The struggle for Turkish economic favours is therefore keen. Turkey is a substantial exporter of tobacco, foodstuffs, chrome ore, lead, and zinc; and her cultivation of cotton has developed so rapidly that the German authorities have offered to buy the entire Turkish export of that staple. On the other hand, there seems little doubt that Turkey's political attitude is one of greater friendliness towards Britain and France, one of shrewd realism towards Italy—of whose naval measures in the Ægean she is as distrustful as Greece—and towards Germany.

(viii) *Destiny Indivisible*

Throughout the last century Europe was racked by convulsions in Central and South-eastern Europe. The cause of these convulsions, which unloosed six European wars, was the Eastern Question: To which Great Power should fall the reversion of the Turkish Empire? The slogan " The Balkan Peninsula for the Balkan peoples " actually resulted in the gradual Balkanization of all Europe; and the Great War was the result of unresolved claims, unreconciled ambitions, among the Great European Powers.

As that war drew to its terrible close it was hoped and believed that a combination of democratic institutions and national self-determination—the twin principles for which so much idealism had been disillusioned and so much blood shed—would buttress the small nations of Central Europe, from the Baltic to the Ægean Sea, against the overweening pretensions of Great Powers. It was thought that the institution of an internationally collective security, safeguarding the rights of national minorities, themselves inevitable however the map of Central Europe be drawn and redrawn, would in turn safeguard Europe entire from another visitation of Armageddon.

But, whatever the reasons—and they cannot be simple or universally valid—democratic institutions went down like ninepins; economic security vanished with collective security; and the small nations of Europe beyond the Rhine and Alps fell over themselves in their haste to take unto themselves big and powerful protectors. All Europe seemed, within a few years of the halcyon year 1929, to have turned into one anarchic feudal state. As in the chaos which succeeded the barbarian conquest of the Western Roman Empire a millennium earlier, small peoples 'commended' themselves for safety to greater; the destruction of a common canon law and order resulted in arbitrary rule and justice; and the worst features of the Dark Ages became familiar happenings—assassinations, beheadings, serfdom, the Ghetto, banditry, piracy, expropriation without process of law. Indeed, the Dark Ages seemed almost bright by comparison. At least they had respect for religion.

This welter of war-in-all-but-name descended upon that portion of the globe which has been wont to call itself the most civilized. In the twentieth century, within twenty years of the war to end wars, there was scarcely a section of the Continent, from west to east, from north to south, in which either a war or the threat of one was not paralysing men's souls with fear. The highest ingenuity of which men's minds were capable was bent to devise more efficient engines of destruction; and more of each nation's labour and resources each year was being put out, not to increase material welfare, but to pile up such engines, which consequently claimed more and more of each nation's output for their nurture and maintenance. Democracy, shivering on the northern and western confines of the Continent, gathered her skirts about her, and hoped, at the best, to be unmolested. And the last word on self-determination was said at Munich.

The wind of change reached hurricane force in 1938. It whipped Austria off the map of Europe, and blew Czecho-Slovakia to pieces. Its violence had not abated when 1939 dawned. It threatened to turn into the tornado of general war.

All this occurred because Europe and its peoples are not just a map; not a game with interchangeable pieces, which one can set up, and play, and win or lose, and then start again, all in a friendly atmosphere. They are, for better or worse, for richer or poorer, a single organism. Once that organism loses a faculty—as it lost the unity of Roman administration and law—it becomes a different organism. The Roman Europe was lost for good, and was never recreated. Hence the concept of the balance of power.

Now, the European balance of power in our own day has been violently upset again. The weakness of twentieth-century Europe will, it is now safe to say, prove to have been the political structure of the Danubian Basin after the last war. The elimination of the Austro-Hungarian Monarchy and its dual administration provided a renascent Germany with a new Continental empire. The Central European bastions fell before German assaults; and it was the fear of such a collapse which led a nineteenth-century Bohemian historian to say that if Austria had not existed then it would have been necessary to invent her.

In 1938 the German Reich gained indisputable advantages. But it was a peculiar Reich which gained them.

It was an empire of 80,000,000 souls, politically policed, militarily disciplined, economically organized for the sacrificial efficiency of war rather than for the delectable blessings of peace. A new theory of economics, born of that economic nationalism which found its first home in the Prussia of 1800, declared to all Germans that the totalitarian state requires behind its diplomacy the strength of totalitarian war, even if only as a threat, and that such war requires the entire resources of the nation, the 'folk,' to be kept in perpetual readiness for the event. Yet in 1938 the Third Reich was greater than any so-called German Reich since the Middle Ages. It had certainly been able to achieve its successes by the mere threat of war; but against whom? Austria? Czecho-Slovakia? Not only against these, but in reality against the last representatives of the older order in Europe; against the two great Western Empires, to whose disadvantage, primarily, any violent and extensive upset of the European balance would redound; against Britain and France.

Now, neither Britain nor France nursed aggressive intentions towards any European state after 1925. Vindictive, perhaps; over-suspicious, perhaps. But not even the France of Poincaré really wanted to attack Germany in future, however shortsightedly the French may have acted in trying to 'squeeze' the Ruhr for reparations. Yet by the end of 1938 the Third Reich and Italy together, linked by land as they had long been linked in the attitude and policy of their Leaders towards the Western Powers, had contrived virtually to cut off Britain and France from any landward, and in time of war perhaps any seaward, connexion with all Europe beyond the western frontiers of the two Axis Powers.

Behind the western front of this Axis, however, the disposition of advantages and forces between the Reich and Italy was very uneven. At Munich Italy was made more economically and militarily dependent on the Reich. At Vienna, a month later, she was forced to align her policy towards Poland and Hungary in keeping with that of Germany. At Munich Italy obtained nothing. In return for what she gave at both Munich and Vienna the German Party-State agreed to support Italian designs in Spain and French North Africa; and the German controlled Press promptly showed that support in December. At the very end of November it was learned that the Reich, Italy, and Japan had concluded a ten-year consultative, military, and economic alliance, providing that in case *two or three* of the members are " engaged in war " they should prosecute it to whatever end in common. It was further learned that this treaty was not to be signed until after the conclusion of a proposed Anglo-Italian accord. Throughout the period immediately after Munich the German Press, the Nazi oligarchs, and the Führer himself were engaged in a dual game of soothing France and ruffling England. Simultaneously, from the other end of the Axis, the Italian Press, Signor Mussolini, and Count Ciano were engaged, with the help of well-drilled crowds and Parliamentary deputies, in ruffling France while they soothed England. The German authorities denigrated British politicians, and went so far as to attempt to dictate what should be alike the composition of the next British Cabinet and the composition of the British Prime Minister's speeches. They claimed the return of colonies, and simultaneously unleashed such a wave of anti-Semitism as appalled the vestigial conscience of the remaining civilized world. The Italian authorities kept up a running fire of claims to Tunis, North Africa, Corsica, Nice, and demanded control of Djibuti besides a share in the control of the Suez Canal.

At the same time, however, Germany was pressing eastward and south-eastward in Europe—against Poland, Danzig, Memel, the new Czecho-Slovakia, Hungary, and Rumania. A Nazi diplomat whose activities in the German Legation in Prague until 1935 had much to do with the earlier organization of Herr Henlein's party was reported in November 1938 to be equally active in his new post in Berne. Switzerland was advised by Nazi technical economic journals at the same time to redirect her trade and investments towards the new South-eastern Europe. In Jugoslavia German influence after Munich made inroads to the disadvantage of Italy. Yet not one derogatory mention was made by Herr Hitler or any of his closest associates after Munich about ' Bolshevik ' Russia.

What are we to conclude from these European after-effects of Munich? When we read them in conjunction with the facts already in our minds whither do they point?

Three results emerge at once. First, the Third Reich has reserved no place in Eastern, Central, and South-eastern Europe for Italy, save that of a poor relation. This vast tract of Europe is to be the new Continental Empire of the Third Reich.   Secondly, Italy is to be compensated, as Bismarck ' compensated ' France after 1870 by supporting her in North Africa against Britain, by Reich support for Italy's claims on Britain and France—in Spain, the Balearics, North Africa, Corsica, Djibuti, the Suez Canal Board, and anywhere else outside Germany's new domain.   Thirdly, both ends of the Axis are to be utilized for simultaneous soothing and ruffling of Britain and France respectively.   By this third method it is doubtless hoped that British statesmen may come to believe that, after Austria and Czecho-Slovakia, France might as well be required to pay future prices for European peace—in Alsace-Lorraine or the Mediterranean or North Africa.

The next questions we must ask are: Do the after-effects of Munich suggest that the two Axis Powers intend joint war against the west?   If so, can they win?   If not, to what is their policy in Europe directed?

Apart from the undeniable psychological antipathies which subsist between Germans and Italians, since Munich their destinies are intertwined, for either state separately cannot hope to hold what it has already secured, territorially, strategically, or economically, without the other's aid and succour.   They can, however, only intend joint war against Britain or France, or both, if they are absolutely confident of a crushing and complete victory within a few months.   Beyond those few months the economic factors already mentioned will operate with cumulative force in favour of the Western Powers, to the disadvantage of Germany and Italy.   This confidence cannot be gauged or prophesied.   It may be the confidence of a desperate gambler, and equally misplaced; it cannot lead to victory, however, unless many other factors operate in favour of Germany and Italy. For example, if Britain and France try to make their own separate terms with either of the Axis Powers, thus allowing themselves to be picked off singly; or if neither Britain nor France rearm, sufficiently rapidly and extensively; or if Germany and Italy together can so organize their economic resources, behind the western front of the Rome-Berlin Axis, as to defy the joint naval blockade of the French and British fleets for long enough to sicken every European with modern warfare.

Thus, apart from passive British and French acquiescence under the mere threat of war, if the two Axis Powers intend in the immediate future a war against the two Western Powers they must win a ' lightning war '; and if it is to be delayed long enough to allow the dominant Axis partner, Germany, to build up and organize for war the economic resources of its new dominions, then the two Axis partners will have to face vast economic difficulties, will have to take a very long time to prepare, and will finally have to face perhaps two years of modern warfare at the end of it. Whatever else might happen to other countries, the régimes of Italy and Germany would not last two years of modern warfare; so that no one would win.

Consequently the Axis Powers together can only be reasonably—though they can always be unreasonably—sure of winning a sudden, cheap war against the two Western Powers. When can they unleash it? At almost any moment. But if they now do so they cannot rely on these vitally important factors: Italian control of the entire Mediterranean, dependability of the Slav and Magyar dominions on the new Reich, and, finally, adequacy of economic strength inside their countries and of supplies from beyond their borders. However one faces these terrible possibilities, one is driven back to the strategic and economic importance of Eastern, Central, and South-eastern Europe. For Germany in 1938 became the dominant partner on the Rome-Berlin Axis; and her interest, her time-table for war, cannot be the same as those of Italy. The Reich must subjugate larger regions of the Europe that lies beyond even its present borders before it can so organize its military and economic resources as to be invulnerable to blockade or attack. And it cannot be rushed by Italy into a general European war—which a war with the west would assuredly be—until it has accomplished this task. If and when the task is accomplished the Reich, with Italy or without her, will be strong enough to be able to choose in which direction it will strike—east or west. Till then rolling up the map of Europe beyond Germany is the immediate problem before the Reich; and no Italian aims or considerations dare be allowed to interfere with the German strategy.

Meanwhile the Axis itself is an admirable diplomatic apparatus for setting France and Britain at loggerheads, securing the isolation of France, the use of Spain and perhaps part of North Africa, and the isolation of all Europe beyond the Rhine and the Alps as a predominantly German dominion.

And that is the crux of the entire problem bequeathed

to Europe by the annexation of Austria and the Munich Settlement. Does it lie in Germany's power alone to organize and exploit this new Danubian dominion, so that at some later day an even Greater Reich can choose in which direction it will dictate Europe's destiny? Can the Reich of early 1939 spare the time, energy, and resources to build up an unassailable position behind the Axis? Or do the leaders of that Reich already realize the inability of their country's present structure to stand that strain? Finally, if they do realize it are they going to stake their all on an immediate gamble for the hegemony of Europe? Are they, like Catilina, preparing desperately to risk all or bring all down in the general ruin?

In December 1938 it was known that the inner councils of the Nazi Party were divided on these questions. The German Army and Air Force were told to prepare for active operations as early as February 1939; all leave was stopped after January 14, 1939; and the German armed forces were organized in such a way that a sixth Army Group, to hold the western front, was established in November 1938, while two other Army Groups were detailed for operations " elsewhere." On the economic side the British plan, announced in December 1938, to increase the facilities for ' export credits ' by 50 per cent. and to add a further 10 per cent. to meet politically subsidized trade in foreign markets caused consternation in the Reich. Its advent so soon after the signing of the Anglo-American Trade Agreement, which itself was an open derogation from the economic isolationism of the 1932 Ottawa Agreements, was a stern warning to the Reich of the magnitude of the financial resources ultimately involved. The visit of Dr Schacht, President of the Reichsbank, to the Governor of the Bank of England, Mr Montagu Norman, in December 1938 was said to be connected with a plan to secure additional exports and free foreign exchange for the Reich, against release of Jewish property from Germany to the same amount.

In any case, the magnitude of the purely economic task facing a Reich woefully short of liquid capital could not be gainsaid. It was out of the question that the Reich and Italy, unless their Leaders were really out of their minds, should deliberately pick a quarrel with Britain and France on any pretext, and rush to war in the hope of sudden and complete victory. Quite apart from the strategic factors already examined (see pp. 70–104), the inconclusiveness of aerial frightfulness, the greater advantage in mechanical apparatus of warfare for the defensive, the lessened importance of man-power, British and French statesmen still have it in their power to turn back upon Germany and Italy the consequences of these latter Powers' economic methods. For example, the Axis Powers are both compelled to recur to 'grabbing' some new material acquisition at successively shorter intervals. The reason for this is that hitherto neither the Reich nor Italy has really organized any solid or sound economic development of its new territories. Such organization requires much capital, much civil labour, and a long time for development. Germany, to whom has fallen the great gains of 1938, has traded for five years in the Danubian and Balkan regions on a reputation built up by another Germany; her recent methods have antagonized old, and not endeared new clients; the system she has adopted is spurious, unreliable for war-time, and not too dependable, as we have seen, for a protracted peace. A rapidly mounting domestic debt, the absence of available liquid funds, compulsory sequestration of religious communities' funds and property, offers to Czecho-Slovakia to employ 150,000 refugee Czechs in the Reich, continuous shortages of foodstuffs, continual deterioration in the quality of manufactures— this is the economic picture of the greater Third Reich in January 1939. That Reich has not stopped once in the last five years seriously to organize its gains for future economic development. Instead, so great was the velocity of its onward rush, it consumed every new gain in a few months, stripped and despoiled all its new resources as quickly as it obtained them. This kind of economic freebooting naturally impelled it to seek for ever wider fields. And that is the danger to all Europe, but principally to Europe beyond Germany, that lies at the heart of the Reich's predatory economy.

It is, perhaps, of interest to note the following extract from the " Introductory Lecture on Political Economy " delivered before the University of Oxford on December 6, 1826—eleven years after Waterloo—by the first Professor of Political Economy there, Nassau Senior:

> Men who fancy they are applying common sense to questions of Political Economy are often applying to them only common prejudice. Instead of opposing, as they fancy, experience to theory, they are opposing the theory of a barbarous age to the theory and experience

of an enlightened one. There never was a man of stronger common sense . . . than Napoleon. He had an utter horror of Political Economy; the principles of which, he said, if an empire were built of granite, would grind it to powder. On such subjects he trusted to common sense. And his common sense was an un-distinguishing acceptance of the whole theory of the mercantile system.

The economic theories of militant dictators have not altered in more than a century. The Third Reich and Italy, like Napoleon, have to try to turn all Europe behind their western borders into a vast arsenal, store-house, and granary. If they do not quietly and methodi-cally set to work and accomplish this during the next few years they will inevitably have to depend upon the extremely undependable lightning war to mould the destinies of the Continent. Yet if they do set about this immense task it will force them to slow down the *tempo* of their domestic and foreign policies, political, military, and economic. It is a grievous dilemma.

Beyond the Rhine and the Alps the fate of all Europe, western and eastern, lies in the hands of those responsible for the destinies of the Third Reich. The purposes for which these men shape the New Danubia will indicate what *rôle* is reserved for the other Great Powers of Europe—for Italy no less than for Britain, France, and Russia. It may be that the oligarchs of the Third Reich will look upon the immediate booty of 1938 as the final instalment of a war fund, and proceed to attack the west for more booty. Terrible as that would be for a short time, we have given reasons for believing that it would speedily fail. The sooner it begins, the quicker it will fail, for the less adequate are the Third Reich's and Italy's resources for a sustained effort. The real danger to Europe—and it is an equally terrible thing to say—is not so much an immediate European war as a continuation of the kind of thing which has been called peace these last five years. If we can secure and buttress real peace in Europe let us do so; but let it be a peace founded on good faith and collaboration, not a peace which is mere absence of general war, while all the moral and strategic positions are lost to an unmoral but strategic opponent. If we cannot ensue the right kind of peace we may be sure that what is being forged on the anvils of the Third Reich since Munich will turn out to be European, not merely Danubian, destiny. The longer it is forged, the harder it will be.

It is not the purpose of this essay to draft or advocate a policy for any particular European Power. But three points are worth making as a conclusion.

First, the Western Powers and their Empires have the resources and the means to rearm as extensively and efficiently as the Third Reich and Italy—perhaps more so. They have the economic advantage; they lack either the will or the ability to utilize it. Secondly, democracies can be as effective as dictatorships—but only if they oppose the despotic oligarchies of the dictatorships by a voluntary and democratic totalitarianism—that is, if they completely close their domestic ranks. This, of course, presupposes the adoption of a completely national foreign policy and defence system. Lastly, neither the political nor the economic diplomacy of the much-vaunted totalitarian states is really efficient. It is cumbrous, costly, and so over-complicated, over-refined, that it often defeats its own ends. If a firmly devised, firmly executed political and economic diplomacy were opposed to it then there could be no doubt, especially after Munich, where the balance of advantage would lie.

It would be mistaken, therefore, to think of all Europe beyond Germany as being from now onward wholly at Germany's disposal. It is not just a repository from which resources can be squeezed without payment; not a far-away region to which German, and perhaps Italian, air-bases and strategic industries may be removed for ultimately safer location. It is a collection of peoples, of nations, of living, sentient human beings; of as many millions as dwell in the Third Reich and Italy together. In the history of Europe the peoples to the south and east of Germany have already played notable parts. They can do so again. There are over 100,000,000 of them between Germany and Russia. Whether the German and Italian oligarchies begin ruthlessly to organize these 100,000,000 people and their resources or not, they oppose Germany and Italy on one side, as do France and Britain on the other. They need not be able to shoot in order to be powerful friends to the two Western Powers. Men who grumble, who dislike alien interference, who must be watched to ensure their allegiances, who yield their services grudgingly—such men can be dangerous to Germany and Italy. They can be more dangerously potent, perhaps, in war than in peace; and more potent in a future war than in any that is past.

It is with the millions of such men in Central and

South-eastern Europe, whose ancestors destroyed both the imagined and the real Central European empires of the past, that the new arbiters of Danubian destiny hope to shape that of Europe. These arbiters may have all the political apparatus. But as yet they have not the material, nor the men, for so ambitious an undertaking. If their enterprise is successful it will not be due to their own merits. It will be because of their opponents' shortcomings.

INDEX